INDIAN FAIRY STORIES

by
Donald A. Mackenzie

PILGRIMS PUBLISHING
◆ Varanasi ◆

INDIAN FAIRY STORIES
Donald A. Mackenzie

Published by:
PILGRIMS PUBLISHING

An imprint of:
PILGRIMS BOOK HOUSE
(Distributors in India)
B 27/98 A-8, Nawabganj Road
Durga Kund, Varanasi-221010, India
Tel: 91-542-2314059, 2314060, 2312456
Fax: 91-542-2312788, 2311612
E-mail: pilgrims@satyam.net.in
Website: www.pilgrimsbooks.com

PILGRIMS BOOK HOUSE (New Delhi)
9 Netaji Subhash Marg, 2nd Floor
Near Neeru Hotel,
Daryaganj,
New Delhi 110002
Tel: 91-11-23285081
E-mail: pilgrim@del2.vsnl.net.in

Distributed in Nepal by:
PILGRIMS BOOK HOUSE
P O Box 3872, Thamel,
Kathmandu, Nepal
Tel: 977-1-4424942
Fax: 977-1-4424943
E-mail: pilgrims@wlink.com.np

Edited by Christopher N Burchett
Cover design by Sasya
Layout by Asha Mishra

ISBN: 81-7769-121-X
Rs.

Printed in India

CONTENTS

INTRODUCTION TO THE NEW EDITION

The tradition of the fairy tale goes way back into the darkest recesses in time. It is a phenomenon, which truly has no beginning or an end. The styles may change also the name of the author but the content follows a similar pattern the triumph of good over evil. The Indian subcontinent having hosted one of the most ancient of civilizations has also been the most prolific in producing these tales. These tales that in one form or another have become loved the world over even though the characters may have slightly different names or the stories being given more recognizable locations.

Most famous of the tales that have come out of the subcontinent are the Jataka tales or Buddha birth stories, the Panchatantra or animal tales and of course the two major epics the Ramayana and the Mahabharata. There are many others, which include the Parrot tales and the tales of Vikramaditya and the Ghost as well as the Ocean of Tales. The last three mentioned are of a later date but the first four come from the ageless depths of the Indian civilization.

Originally of course these tales were used by the religious leaders of the times to instill a moral and religious code into the lives of their followers and also have the honour of forming the mythical basis for the origins of the Hindu pantheon of gods and demi-gods. The hidden poignant message of these stories has carried on down through the ages and still form a base for putting children on the right course for becoming upright and worthwhile citizens.

Even in the twentieth century authors like J R R Tolkein and Mervyn Peake have gone back to the depths of our unknown origins to create an immortal myth not only to entertain but to educate and instill in humankind the values of humanity as well. All such tales have over the ages not only entertained but have generally brought out the best in all of us. They have created a much greater understanding of those less fortunate than ourselves the story of the little matchbox seller in the Hans Christian Anderson collection coming foremost to mind.

This particular collection of tales is a fusion of all that is best in the great gamut of Indian tales. It is a collection that portrays the fine balance and sensibility that exists between humankind and the lesser creatures that surround them. It displays the fine sense that these creatures infuse in the persons that they come in contact with. Proving that many of the greatest moral truths may be gained by a careful study of the ways of the animal kingdom. It also shows that no creature is too small or insignificant to be ignored.

Christopher N Burchett
July 2001.
VARANASI.

THE PERILS OF AMBITION

There is a beautiful mountain is northern India, which was called Gandhamadana. It is entirely overgrown with trees and shrubs, and its quiet solitudes are haunted by those beautiful spirit beings the fair Siddhas and the music-loving Gandharvas.

Once a number of Brahmans and hunters visited this mountain. The Brahmans made search for medicinal herds is secret places of which they had knowledge, and when they found them, discussed their virtues with one another, as is their wont. It was by these wise and holy men that the hunters were informed of one of secrets of the mountain. There is a deep cave there, which is situated on the face of a steep and dangerous precipice, and in the cave there is a jar, and in the jar a goodly quantity of honey of bright yellow hue. But the honey contained in the jar is of no ordinary kind. It is, indeed, the favorite drink of the god Kubera, the guardian of Celestial treasure, and is possessed of rare virtues. He who drinks of it will become immortal; it will restore the eyesight of the blind, and make youthful the elderly once again. But the honey is not obtainable by human beings, for the jar within the cave is guarded constantly by snakes whose poison is exceedingly virulent. The Brahmans duly warned the hunters regarding these fierce and all-powerful snake guardians.

But the hunters were stricken with the desire to obtain a portion of the drink of Kubera. They climbed the cliff and found the cave, and saw the snake-protected jar. Despite the warnings of the wise Brahmans, who had knowledge of things beyond the reach of ordinary men, they resolved to obtain it. What their eyes beheld and their hearts desired, it seemed to them they could seize with their hands. One by one the hunters darted forward to grasp the jar, and one by one they perished in that cave which was full of virulent snakes.

So does the ambitious man desires to gain possession of the whole earth without a rival. He sees the honey, but in his folly does not realize the inevitable and terrible fate which awaits him.

THE PRINCE AND THE MAGICIAN

A long time ago there lived a king and a queen who had great wealth. Their country was prosperous, and the people lived happily. In their gorgeous palace the both had everything their hearts could desire, except one thing, and that was a son. But at length a son was born, and then there was much rejoicing in the kingdom.

The young prince was called Chandra, and he was comely and sweet to behold. So greatly was he beloved by the queen that she would never allow him to be out of her sight by day, and he slept in her arms he whole night long. Tenderly cared for, the child grew and prospered until he was a year old. On his first birthday the king gave a great feast, and the people decorated the city with banners and garlands of flowers.

There never was a great and good man who had not an enemy. A great robber, who lived in the midst of a deep forest on the outskirts of the kingdom, hated the king because he was so well loved by his people and enjoyed all happiness that life could bring. So this robber resolved to make the king the most miserable man upon earth, because he himself was greatly hated and could not, although he was possessed of much wealth, obtain any happiness at all. He was a magician who had derived his power and the secrets of his art by selling his soul to the King of the Daityas (demons). Thinking ever of the fate which was in store for him when he had lived his life, he was ever apprehensive and gloomy.

It chanced that when the people were rejoicing on the first birthday of the child prince, the robber disguised himself as a holy man and went to the king's palace. He carried in his right hand a necklace of pearls, and he asked the guards to permit him to enter so that he might present it to the king as a gift for his son and heir. He was allowed to pass through the gate. Then he walked into the palace and laid the beautiful gift at the feet of the king as he sat on his throne surrounded by many great and noble lords. The pearls shone with the brightness of stars, and dazzled the eyes of everyone who saw them.

"Where do you come from?" asked the king, as the man prostrated himself on the floor.

"I have come from the kingdoPm of wide waters," answered the robber lord, "and this necklace I obtained from the queen of the golden cave. Now, know that it has special virtues. The child who wears it will become the wisest and most powerful warrior in the world."

The king thanked the man for the gift, and ordered his servants to give him food in abundance and many pieces of gold, and, indeed, to grant him whatever wish he desired.

Said the robber lord: "My only food is roots and herbs, and I desire not to feast in the palace. Nor have I any love of wealth. But, O king, you would honor me, grant but one favor. Permit me to see the young prince before my eyes close in death."

His wise was granted, and the robber lord was led to the chamber in which the queen sat nursing her well-loved child.

Never before had he beheld a more beautiful and happier woman, and he said to himself: "Now I know why the king derives such great joy in life. If this woman were my wife, I should rejoice in her love, and I would be miserable as I am."

It had been his intention to cast a spell upon the child so that he might never live to wear the pearl necklace, but his mind his become so greatly occupied with the queen that he forgot the purpose of his mission.

· So he sat down to talk with her. When he had blessed the child and praised him, the queen smiled upon him, and he thought her smile was more beautiful than moonlight on the mountains. Her voice sounded in his ears like the song of birds; her laughter was sweeter than the plashing of a small crystal stream.

"I shall carry her away at once," thought the wild and wicked robber lord.

He drew from beneath his single garment a magic wand and waved it once, whereupon all the attendants fell into a deep slumber; he waved it twice, and the queen was transformed into a small black dog; he waved it a third time, and the dog fell asleep. Then he left the chamber, closing the door behind him, and passed out of the palace and through the gates, and then through the city, carrying the small black dog in his arms. He walked on until he reached a deep forest. Having waved his wand, he was immediately transported through the air to his stronghold. "I will shut up the queen in my high tower," said the robber lord, "until she consents to become my life."

Soon after the robber lord left the palace, the Rajah went towards the chamber in which the young prince lay, so that he might show the beautiful pearl necklace to the queen. He was greatly astonished to find all the waiting-women lying on the floor fast asleep. The child, he saw, was asleep also. But what made him wonder most was that he could not see the queen anywhere. He passed from chamber to chamber looking for her, but he looked in vain. Meanwhile the waiting-women continued to slumber and could not be awakened.

At length the king returned to the chamber in which the Rani had sat. He knelt beside the child, and laid his right hand upon his forehead. As he did so one of the pearls touched the child's face, and immediately he woke up and smiled. When the king discovered that there were secret virtues in the necklace, he touched the faces of each of the slumbering attendants with it, and one after another they woke up as the child had done.

Trembling, he asked of them: "Where is the queen?" But they were unable to tell him. "O my lord," said the elder attendant, "we know nothing of what has happened here since the holy man waved his small black wand in the air. Sleep fell upon us immediately, and with sleep came forgetfulness.

The king next spoke to the guards who stood at the entrance of the palace, and asked if they had seen the holy man; and they answered: "We saw him entering the palace with a bright pearl necklace in his hand, and while leaving, carrying a small black dog which slumbered in his arms."

Then the king knew that the holy man was a magician in disguise who had carried away the beautiful queen whom he loved. Great was his sorrow. He rent his robes and gave himself up to despair.

After this the king sent forth warriors to search everywhere for the missing queen, but none of them ever returned again. He had six brothers, and one after the other they vanished from sight and knowledge. The king was then the most miserable man upon earth.

So year after year the king lamented, and year after year brave warriors went forth in quest of the queen, but all in vain. At length, when fourteen years had gone past, the king said: "She will never again return, and I have now no desire to live any longer." He mourned, and all his people mourned with him.

By this time the prince Chandra had grown up to be a brave youth. And one day he was told by his grandmother how a magician had come to the palace with the gift of a pearl necklace, and had carried away the beautiful queen, his mother.

Then Chandra stood before his father and said, " If you will give me the pearl necklace which the magician presented to you so that I might wear it, I will go forth and search for my lost mother."

At first the king refused to bring forth the necklace from its hiding-place, fearing that it would injure his son, but at length he was prevailed upon to give it unto him. When he received it, Chandra placed it round his neck. As soon as he did so, he was completely transformed. He was no longer a boy, but a strong warrior, and great wisdom beyond his years appeared in his face. When he spoke, his voice was the voice of a lord who compelled obedience.

"Now, I will go forth alone," he said, "nor will I return until I bring my mother with me."

When he had spoken thus, the king blessed him and permitted him to depart. Although his heart was filled with confidence, yet he spoke no words of hope.

Chandra left the city, and many of the people followed him to the forest, watching from a distance, but the prince advanced boldly and without fear, and the fierce man-eater turned from his path and fled away. When this happening was made known to the king, that sorrowful monarch said: "It is good omen, but greater perils must yet be overcome."

The prince wandered on, and the people feared to follow any farther. He passed through the forest, and crossed a wide plain, and then ascended the slopes of a steep plain, and then ascended the slopes of a steep mountain which was covered with trees. At length he felt weary and lay down to sleep. How long he slept he knew not, but suddenly he found himself awakened by a low hissing sound. He looked towards the place from where the sound should came, and beheld a great black serpent creeping up the trunk of an old tree towards an eagle's nest. The young eagles saw the reptile approach, and began to cry for help. Chandra at once sprang a single step forward and drawing his sword, smote the serpent a single blow which wavered its body. Its coils were unloosed from the tree, and the two and the two parts of the long, black body fell upon the ground and wriggled about for a time. Chandra looked on with wonder, for it seemed that the reptile still lived. Then he saw the two portions coming together and uniting. When that happened the serpent became whole again, and once more turned towards the tree. Chandra drew his sword again and cut the black monster into three parts, but these also came together. Then he cut off the head and rolled it away a great distance from the body, and dug a hole with his sword and buried it. After that the serpent body lay quite still, and ants came to devour it.

No sooner was the serpent slain than the mother eagle and the father eagle returned to their nest. When they perceived that Chandra had protected their young they said: "You are the strong and wise prince of whom our grandsire prophesied, saying, 'He will be your deliverer'. This ferocious black serpent has constantly devoured our young ones, but now he will not persecute us any more. O prince, when you have need of our aid, you summon us and we shall obey you willingly."
Edited up to here

Chandra thanked the eagles and went on his way. After traveling a great distance he lay down again to sleep, and slept for many hours. When he woke up he heard a low wailing cry, and he rose and went towards the place from where it came. He found a wild deer with its horns caught in a thicket, and he saw tears falling from its eyes as it wailed. Drawing his sword he cut the thicket asunder and released the noble animal. Then the deer spoke to him: "A good action deserves a generous reward. You have rescued me from death, for before long a lion would have found me here and devoured me. If ever you need my help summon me, and I. shall at once hasten to serve you. I am the most nimble-footed deer in the world and my flight is as swift as thought."

Chandra thanked the deer and went on his way. At length he approached a house, just when darkness was coming on, and he went towards it and entered. Sitting alone in the one room he saw an old woman. As he approached her, she lifted up her eyes and said, "Beautiful youth, are you not afraid to come here? This is the house of my son, the gardener, who serves the robber lord. The robber lord is a great magician, and if he sees you he will transform you into a stone or a tree, as he has already done to many noble men who have searched for the beautiful queen."

When the prince heard the words his heart leaped with delight within him, and he said: "it is because you have a kindly heart that you have spoken to me words of warning. I am therefore moved with love towards you. And I know that because your heart is kindly you will shield me from harm."

" Who are you?" the woman asked.

"I am the son of the queen who was taken away by the great magician," Chandra answered. "My father, the king, has grown old sorrowing for her. I was but one year old when my mother, the queen, was transformed into a small black dog and carried from the palace by this wicked man. I still remember her because very month she comes to me in dreams, sometimes smiling upon me and sometimes weeping bitterly."

"Ever does she lament for you," the woman said; "and I know well that you are her son and no deceiver, because she has told me that once every month she has visions of you in her dreams."

The woman gave the prince food to eat, and then disguised him by dressing him as a girl. And a comely girl he seemed. When her son came home, he asked: "Who is this young woman?"

"She is my sister's daughter," the other told him. "Her mother and father and dead, and she will dwell with us here until her rich friends come for her."

Said the son: "If the robber lord sees her he may put her to death."

The woman answered: "Leave everything to me, and I will speak to your lord on her behalf."

Next morning Chandra walked through the garden with the old woman. And when the robber lord came at night the woman approached him saying: "My sister's daughter has came to dwell with me. She has knowledge of a secret love charm, and can find the herb which, if it is tasted by a woman, will cause her to love the first man she sees more dearly than life itself."

Said the robber lord: "This girl hath knowledge which I do mot possess. I cannot cause my beautiful prisoner to love me. Tell your niece to find the love herb and bring it to me."

"The herb must be given to the queen by the girl herself," said the old woman. "She must visit her first and win her confidence."

Said the robber lord: "Then let her go to the tower with beautiful flowers every day, so that the queen may learn to desire her company."

So was the matter arranged. Chandra, disguised as a girl, went to the tower next morning. The queen gazed upon him with loving eyes, and said: "The sight of you is dear to me, for you are so like to my son whom I see in my dreams."

Chandra then made himself known to his mother, and she embraced him and wept over him.

"I have come to set you free," Chandra said, " and if you will do as I advise, then the wicked magician will be overthrown."

Each morning mother and son were together, and at length the time came when Chandra said: "When the robber lord comes next to speak to you, say you will consent to marry him if he will but give you a little time to ponder over the matter. His attitude towards you will immediately change. Then try to discover the secret of his power, and how he can be put to death."

The queen consented to do as her son advised her, and then Chandra informed the magician that his prisoner had tasted the love herb. Immediately the wicked man hastened to the tower. His heart leapt within him when the queen smiled upon him and said she would marry him.

It was his advice that the wedding should take place without delay; but his beautiful prisoner said: " We must wait a little longer yet, and you must prove your love for me by giving me your confidence."

He promised to do this, and she asked him: "Are you immortal? Can no one put you to death? Art you so great a magician that no one can cause you an injury?"

The robber lord looked in her eyes steadily and said: "Why do you want me to reveal my secrets?"

Said the queen: "It is but right that a woman should possess her lord's secrets, so that if danger threatens him she may know how to protect him."

The magician was deceived by her answer, and informed her that his life depended on the life of a green parrot which was cared for by Rakshasas[1](The Rakshasas were a kind of demons or evil beings, hostile to man.) in the midst of a deep forest. "The parrot," he said, "lives in a small grove surrounded by a river of fire if anyone should pass the Rakshasas and attempt to find the parrot, the fire would burn him. Beside the parrot are seven jars of water, and so long as these jars are full, the parrot cannot be lifted up."

The queen smiled and said: "No mortal can ever reach this parrot and destroy your life."

When Chandra next visited the tower, she informed him of all the magician had said. The prince said he would immediately set out to obtain the green parrot.

"Alas! my son," lamented the queen, "if you will undertake this perilous adventure, death will overtake you."

Said Chandra: "By virtue of the pearl necklace, which the magician gifted to me, I shall succeed. Unless I go you will never regain your freedom, nor will my father see you any more, nor will the warriors who have come hither to rescue you regain their forms again, but ever remain as rocks and trees." On that same evening Chandra took his departure. He traveled all night, and when day dawned he thought of the deer which he had rescued from the thicket, and cried out: "I would that the swift deer were with me to give me its help."

No sooner had he spoken thus than the deer came to him and spoke, saying: "Speak your commands so that I may obey them."

Said Chandra: "Carry me to the forest in which lives the green parrot, surrounded by a river of fire and protected by Rakshasas."

The deer said: " Be seated on my back and I will bear you to the edge of the forest."

So Chandra sat on the back of the deer, and the deer scampered away at a great speed. The nimble footed animal ran for three days and three nights without resting. Over hills he went and through forests, over rivers and lakes and across wide plains. At length, at the dawn of the fourth day, the deer halted on the edge of a great forest which resounded with the voices of roaring Rakshasas.

"I will tarry here until you return," the deer said, "but I can go no farther."

"I would that the eagles were here," Chandra said, "for I have need of their assistance."

When he had spoken thus, he heard a rushing sound coming through the air. Before long he saw the eagles. They perched upon a rock and called to him, saying: "What service can we do you, O prince who slew the black serpent?"

Said Chandra: "Bear me to the grove surrounded by a river of fire in which dwells the green parrot."

The eagles said: "Tie a cord to your belt, and we will take the ends of it in our beaks and carry you to the fire-protected grove."

Chandra did as the eagles advised him, and they carried him over the forest and dropped him down in the grove beside the green parrot. First he overthrew the seven jars of water. Then he seized the parrot. As he did so, the Rakshasas began to howl more loudly than ever. But before they could come through the fire Chandra called to the eagles which were hovering above him, and they came down holding the cord in their beaks, until he grasped it and attached it to his belt. Then they flew away with him. Hordes of Rakshasas ran through the forests, following in the direction of the eagles' flight; but Chandra was placed on the back of the deer, and the deer sped away swift as thought before the pursuing monsters could reach him. In time he returned to the domain of the robber lord, the great magician.

Now the magician had knowledge that his life was in peril. Chandra found him standing beside the tower in which his mother was kept a prisoner.

Holding the parrot in his hand the prince addressed him, saying: "Now you must do whatever I command you."

Said the magician: "O wise young man give me that parrot and I will grant you whatever you may ask of me."

"Why do you wish to obtain the parrot?" asked Chandra. "It is a pet bird of mine, and I do not care to part with it."

Said the magician: "Ask of me anything you would possess, and I will grant it if you will promise to give me the parrot." As he spoke he began to walk towards the prince.

"Stand back!" Chandra commended. As he spoke he pulled a father from the bird's tail and flung it on the ground. The magician trembled and stood. "Now," Chandra continued, "first of all, release all the warriors whom you have transformed into rocks and trees."

The magician waved his hand obediently, and immediately warriors sprang up on all sides.

"Now give me the parrot," he wailed.

Chandra laughed. The magician raised his wand again; but the prince pulled off the right wing of the parrot. As he did so, the magician's right arm fell upon the ground. The wicked man seized the wand in his left hand, but Chandra pulled off the left wing of the parrot, and the magician's left arm fell upon the ground also.

"Give me my parrot," wailed the robber lord, who was now unable to injure the prince by waving his magic wand.

"Declard me the possessor of all your wealth," Chandra commended.

"All that I have is yours," was the answer. "Give me my parrot."

"You shall have it," Chandra answered as he twisted the bird's neck and thus slew it. Immediately the magician fell dead upon the ground.

The prince then hastened to the tower and brought forth the queen. He afterwards assembled all the warriors of his country who had been transformed into trees and rocks, and when they had gathered the rich treasure of the magician, they set forth with Chandra and the queen to their own country. Great were the rejoicings in the kingdom when all the lost ones returned. The king became young gain because the queen was restored to him. Nevertheless he gave up the throne to his son, and Chandra ruled over the kingdom wisely and well.

A VAIN CAMEL

A white camel, which was exceedingly vain because of its beauty and strength, one day deserted a caravan, and wandered into a deep forest to search for new company. He had grown weary of his equals, and desired to associate with his superiors. Now the king of the forest was a powerful lion, whose chief advisers were a tiger, a jackal, and a crow. These had taken vows to help one another, and were most intimate friends.

The jackal had just enjoyed an excellent meal, and lived at peace with all living creatures when he met the camel. "Come with me," he said. " and I will present you to the king." So the camel was taken to the lion's den.

"Who are you, and why have you come here?" the king of the forest asked in a pleasant voice.

Said the camel: "I am the whitest camel in the world. All other camels are jealous of me. Being strong and high-spirited, I have no desire to live the same life as those of my kind who serve mankind. Rather would I enjoy the freedom of the forest and have for friends the noble animals who defy human beings. Ever since my childhood I have yearned for high life. I am an excellent fighter and an accomplished talker, and am willing to help and entertain your majesty."

" This fellow is really handsome and pleasant," the lion remarked; "he will make an excellent companion."

"I admire him very much," said the tiger; "I have never seen such a fine neck on any camel."

"His legs are shapely indeed," the jackal commented.

"Have you observed his eves?" asked the crow; "they are large and beautiful."

The camel felt highly flattered, and bowed to the forest rajah and his friends. "I consider myself honored by your friendship," he exclaimed with heartfelt gratitude.

So it was agreed that the camel should become a member of the lion's court. Food was plentiful at the time, and there was nothing the forest animals enjoyed more then good company. The camel was never weary of relating his experiences. And the lion, tiger and jackal were especially interested in his stories about mankind and their doings. They found that his knowledge of human beings was much more intimate and varied than the crow's. Before long the crow became jealous, and one day he spoke to the camel and said: "do you intend to remain here long?"

The camel said: "I will reside permanently at the king's court. One who becomes accustomed to the company of his superiors has no desire to sup again with his inferiors."

Said the crow: "Should you chance to incur the displeasure of the king, it might go hard with you."

"I have no reason to fear anything," the camel answered. "The lion has vowed never to do me harm. A king's word is law."

Said the crow: "He has pledged my safety also."

"What makes me feel doubly safe," the camel remarked, "is that his royal highness enjoys my company so much. I am an excellent talker."

Said the crow: "What makes me feel doubly safe is that I have an excellent pair of wings."

The camel smiled a superior smile, and began to browse on thistles. "It is quite evident," he said to himself, "that the crow is jealous of me and desires to get rid of my presence here. I have completely supplanted him as the chief entertainer of the king."

In the rainy season, the lion became unwell and was unable to hunt. Food grew scarce, and at length the jackal said to the tiger: "Had we better not slay this thistle browser and make an excellent meal?"

Said the tiger: "That idea has already suggested itself to me. But do you think the king will consent to such a thing after pledging the camel's safety?"

The crow remarked: "The lion is weak and hungry. A hungry lion has a short memory."

"Let us consult his royal highness on this matter", the jackal suggested.

Together they went to the lion, and found him lying moaning in his den. "Have you found food for me?" the forest king asked them as soon as they appeared.

The crow shook his head. "May it please your majesty," he said, "we have found no food,"

"Are we to die of starvation?" moaned the lion.

Said the crow: "Your majesty will certainly not starve unless you refuse the food which is offered to you."

The lion looked round and remarked: "What do you mean? I have not refused food, and none has been offered to me"

Then the crow whispered in the lion's car. "The food I refer to," he said, "is the fat white camel."

The lion frowned. "I have pledged my word." He answered sternly, "that no harm should come to the camel. I never break my word. A king's word is his bond. I cannot therefore slay our friend."

Said the crow: "May it please your majesty, I never suggested that you should forget your pledge and slay the camel. But what if the camel should happen to offer himself to you as food would your royal highness refuse such an offer?"

The lion's eyes glistened, and he rose and paced up and down his den impatiently. "I am very hungry," he muttered.

After this, the crow went to search for the camel, and, having found him spoke, saying: "The king is unwell and low-spirited. He believes he has not a faithful friend in the world. That is often the way with invalids: they grow so despondent. Our beloved king sill not be cheered unless his advisers show proof of their loyalty. We all intend therefore to visit him together. We must convince him that we are his unfailing helpers and companions."

"The suggestion is an excellent one," said the camel; " I will go with you and the others to the lion's den."

"Very well," the crow remarked, "we had better depart at once."

"What do you intend to do?" asked the camel as they hastened on their way.

"As for myself," the crow answered him, "I shall just do and say what the others do and say. It is by imitating the noble born that one acquires noble manners."

When they were all gathered together before the lion's den, the tiger stopped and spoke. "Your Majesty, I perceive with sorrow that you are weak and hungry and disconsolate. I pray you therefore that you should devour my poor flesh."

"Dear Tiger," the lion answered, "I would rather die than do such a thing."

The jackal then flung himself on the ground and said: "will it please your royal highness to eat me?"

"No, no," moaned the lion, "I will never eat my faithful jackal."

"Then," said the crow, "your majesty will make a meal of my poor body."

"Ah, my good friend," answered the lion," you touch my heart with your generous offer, and I feel greatly cheered. But I would father die than consent to your proposal.

The camel next stepped forward and, not desiring to seem less loyal than the others, said: "Do me the honor, O mighty king, of breaking your fast upon me."

No sooner had the camel spoken thus, than the tiger leapt upon his neck and tore his throat open. Then lion began to devour his flank, while the jackal seized a leg, and the crow picked out his eyes. Before night fell the camel was completely devoured, and the jackal had collected his bones together to serve him for future meals.

Said the crow: "Nothing will conceal malice so well as courtesy."

"That is true," cried the cedar on which the crow sat. "The flooding river has sung sweetly to me, and kissed me from morning till eventide, and all the time it was undermining my roots. I am now about to fall." Even as it spoke the cedar fell.

The jackal laughed when he saw that the crow was homeless; but that cunning old bird croaked: "I have excellent wings. I will find another tree."

"I hope you will continue to dwell near us," the tiger said, "we enjoy your conversation so much."

"Especially since the camel has chosen to sacrifice himself," moaned the lion. "Alas! we miss our beautiful white friend."

"He was excellent company," the jackal commented; "I think he was a perfect camel.

The crow snapped his beak. "The camel was not without his defects," he said. "For one thing he lacked the sense to know that it is mistake to make rash proposals, lest one should be taken at one's word."

THE FOWLER AND THE BIRDS

A fowler set out his net upon the ground so that he might catch birds. As it chanced, two birds were snared in it; and after struggling for some time, vainly endeavoring to make escape, one said to the other: "You are pulling one way and I am pulling another. Unless we both pull together, we shall never be able to fly away, but will lie exhausted until the fowler comes and puts us to death. Let us unite our efforts, therefore, and by assisting one another not only free ourselves from the net, but carry it away and use it for our own purposes."

The two birds then began to pull together, and before long they loosened the cords and soared high in the air, carrying the net with them. As they did so, the fowler came near. He observed that the birds were flying away. He did not, however, despair on that account, but followed in the direction in which they went.

A devotee who lived in a hermitage had just finished his morning prayers when he met the fowler. Seeing this man running about hither and thither in pursuit of the birds, he said: "O fowler, it seems both strange and wonderful to me that you who are a treader of earth should thus follow after two travelers of the air."

Said the fowler in answer: "These two birds have united their efforts and are carrying way my net. I cannot seize them so long as they agree between themselves. But I an certain that if I wait long enough they will begin to quarrel, and when that happens they will become my prey."

The fowler spoke truly. Before long the birds began to dispute one with another which another which of them should possess the net.

One said: "the net is mine, because I was the one who discovered how it could be carried away. As I have thus saved your life, you are my debtor, and the service you have rendered in assisting me to obtain the net should be regarded as payment to me for rescuing you from the hands of the fowler." said the other bird: "I was the first to enter the net, and have therefore a prior claim to the ownership of it. Besides, I am much stronger than you are. Had you not followed after me, I should have carried away the net without any difficulty. You say you discovered how we should escape. That is ungrateful of you, because all that you really did was to stop struggling against one who is stronger than yourself, and join the winning side."

In this way the birds kept on quarrelling, and neither was able to convince the other regarding its claim to the net. Then they began to struggle while yet in mid-air, pulling in different directions. As a result they soon became so exhausted that they fell to the ground, and the watchful fowler seized them without difficulty and regained possession also of his net.

A wise old bird who witnessed all that happened said: "Most of our troubles are caused by disagreement among ourselves, and disagreement is caused when we behave like mean-minded persons who, having won riches, become avaricious and forget their duties to their fellows. Those who quarrel over their mutual possessions usually find that they have in the end contributed to the prosperity of their enemies."

A FELINE DEVOTEE

Once upon a time a wicked old cat lived on the banks of the Ganges, near to a place where there was a colony of mice. It was unable to catch a sufficient number of mice to satisfy its appetite, for its eyes had grown dim, and it was no longer nimble and swift as in youth. So it said: "I shall certainly grow weaker and weaker and die of starvation unless I can obtain more mice. As I cannot do this by force, it is necessary that I should exercise more cunning. By exercising my special abilities I may win the confidence of the mice and thus be able to deceive them."

The cat then selected a prominent place beside the river, and there imitated a devotee by pretending to abstain from activity. When the mice came near, the wicked animal upraised its paws and said: "I am now practicing virtue and desire no longer to commit any sin."

In time the mice began to praise the cat, believing that their ancient enemy was really engaged in the observance of vows. Then they said: "We have many enemies. Let this cat, therefore, become our maternal uncle, so that our young ones and our old ones may be protected from all harm."

When the mice decided that they should thus trust the old cat they addressed it, saying: "it is our desire that we should be enabled through your grace to go about freely without fear of injury. You are our great friend and a sure refuge. We therefore place ourselves under your protection, because you are now devoted to goodness. Protect us as the wielder of the thunderbolt protects the Celestials."

The cat said: "I do not see why, because I happen now to practice virtue, I should give you the protection you ask for. Nevertheless I cannot avoid doing good. I will therefore grant your request on condition that you will obey my commands. As the vow which I am observing is very severe, I have grown weak and cannot move about from place to place. It is my wish that every day a number of strong mice should carry me down to the riverside. If you promise thus to serve me, I shall be your protector."

The mice answered saying: "So be it. Your desire will be fulfilled." All the mice thus become the servants of the wicked old cat.

Time went past, and the mice served their "uncle" faithfully. But the cat stealthily devoured large numbers, and began to grow plump and strong again.

Then the mice gathered together in secret and said one to another: " it is strange to find that our 'uncle' is daily increasing in strength while our numbers are gradually growing fewer."

They pondered over this; and a wise mouse, whose name was Dindika, said: "Let us all go down together to the river place. I will follow you and stay beside our 'uncle'."

The mice agreed to this, and the cat, not knowing that he was suspected, seized Dindika and ate him. It had been his custom always to devour the last mouse of a company, so that those in front might not see what happened.

When the mice gathered together again in secret, they found that Dindika was missing. A very old mouse, whose name was Kilika, spoke these wise words: "Fellow mice! Our 'uncle' is deceiving us. He hath no desire to practice virtue. Pretending to de our friend, he is really our most dangerous enemy. As Dindika cannot now be seen, it is evident that he is dead and that our 'uncle' has devoured him. Therefore let us keep watch upon him."

The mice then sent out spies to conceal themselves, and they observed that the cat was quite able to walk about, and was in the habit of young going after companies of mice and devouring those which were behind. They therefore warned all their fellows, saying: "He who lives on fruits and berries cannot grow plump and strong. The cat pretends to practice virtue simply for the sake of obtaining rewards. He is thriving and faring well at the expense of the unsuspecting mice."

When the mice heard this, they deserted the cat and said: "it is necessary for our own safety and happiness that we should not repose our trust in an individual whose speech is of one kind and whose conduct is of another."

THE FOOLISH LEADER

There was once a band of monkeys, and the younger members of it revolted against the rule of the monkey king, because they considered that he did not treat them fairly and allow them to do as they pleased. Indeed the young monkeys regarded themselves as much wiser than their elders. So they formed a separate band, and chose a leader who had much to say on all occasions, and was therefore regarded by the un-experienced as a most accomplished person.

One night the leader of these young monkeys looked down from the branch of a tree, and saw the reflection of the moon on the river. He immediately wakened all the others and said: "The time has come when we can distinguish ourselves and prove our wisdom and our worth. I have just discovered that the moon has fallen into the river. Let us pull it out before it is carried away, so that it may fly back again to its proper place."

Said the young monkeys one to another: "Our opportunity has come indeed. Let us rescue the moon while the elder monkeys are asleep, and they will all show us more respect in the future."

For a time they debated how they should proceed to carry out their intention, and at length the leader said: "To reach the moon we should form a monkey rope. By so doing we shall achieve success and will share the credit of rescuing it from the river."

They thought that this was an excellent suggestion. So they began to form the monkey rope. First one monkey suspended himself from the branch of a tree overhanging the river; a second monkey slipped down and hung on to his tail, then a third monkey swung from the tail of the second, and so on unit all the monkeys were formed into a living rope. The leader was the last to come down, and just as he reached out his hands to grasp the moon, the branch snapped and the whole band of young monkeys fell into the river.

When this disaster happened, they shrieked aloud, and the elder monkeys came to their aid. All the young monkeys were rescued by the members of the senior band, except the leader, who was drowned.

When the king of the monkeys was informed how the accident happened, he said: "When the foolish follow a foolish leader they always meet with disaster. Let this be a warning to all young monkeys who forget that their elders are wiser and more experienced than they are."

STORY OF THE OCEAN QUEEN

In times long past there lived a king in the city of SilverGates, and he had no son until he was of great age. When the prince was born his heart was filled with gladness, and he commanded that everything the child desired should be given to him. So it came about that the king's son grew up accustomed to have every wish he had gratified without restraint, and as the years went on he became more and more willful and selfish. A number of servants waited upon him continually, and whatever the prince asked them to obtain for him they went for speedily, and no matter whose property it was, they seized it in the name of the king. Thus the whims of the young prince set law and order at defiance, until in time the people felt that they had nothing that they could call their own. Merchants concealed their precious stones, and children hid away their toys when the king's son passed through the city of Silver Gates carried in his palanquin. Those who carried him feared lest some day he should order them to fly, and have them put to death if they disobeyed him.

It chanced that one day a company of strolling players visited the city of Silver Gates. The young prince saw them, and commanded that they should perform before him in the palace grounds. This they were exceedingly glad to do, believing they would receive generous gifts from the king.

Among the player there was a lad who performed wonderful feats of skill. One of these was particularly pleasing to the young prince. A sharp two-edged sword was flung in the air, and the lad leapt up nimbly and performed a somersault, encircling the falling sword, which would have wounded him to death had he touched it. Twice he performed this dangerous feat. The young prince applauded him each time and said: "Do it once again." But the lad hesitated and said: "O Prince, I must not overtax my strength lest an accident should befall me. The feat is difficult to perform, and if I should miscalculate the distance I must leap, or fail to rise sufficiently high by reason of my strength failing me, the sword would pass through my body, or sever one of my limbs. Tomorrow I shall again gratify your royal wish should such be your desire."

Said the prince: "Perform the feat once again as I have commanded you."

"Alas!" exclaimed the lad, "I am quite unable to do so, but if you will permit me to leap into the river I will go through swimming feats to please your heart."

The young prince grew furious at what the lad said, and turning to his servants said: "Let him be put to death."

Then the servants seized the lad and began to drag him away.

"O spare my son, wise and noble prince." Pleaded the lad's father, an elderly man with long hair and untrimmed beard, clad in a coarse woolen garment and wearing a nose-ring and earrings like those of his king.

The prince looked scornfully upon the man and turned away his head.

Then the distracted father prostrated himself before the king to plead for his son's life.

"It is a law in my kingdom," the king said, "that everyone should obey the commands of the young prince."

Said the player: "Of this we had no knowledge. Would that we had been acquainted with your strange law, for, had we been, we should never have entered the city of Silver Gates. O mighty king! Listen to the world of a far-travelled man. Punish not one who does wrong without knowledge, but rather him who, having knowledge, willingly breaks the law like the mariner who became the husband of Ocean Queen."

Now the king loved well to listen to tales of strange adventures, and had never before heard of this mariner who became the bride of the Ocean Queen; so he said: "I will bid the prince to spare your son's life and in the meantime, you relate to me the doings of this mariner, and if the tale is pleasing to my heart, I shall grant you whatever wish you desire, even if it be the half of my treasure."

Then the servants were commanded to spare the lad's life for a little time while his father told of the mariner "who", he said, "was punished for breaking a law of which he had knowledge" And this was the tale which the old player related:

"O mighty king of the city of Silver Gates, may your days be long and may your wisdom increase with knowledge. Now know that there once lived a daring mariner who crossed the seven seas and the sea beyond, and beheld all the wonders of the deep. It chanced that he was once shipwrecked in a storm. All the other members of the crew perished; he alone was saved, for he swam a great distance through the sea and reached safely a small island which was covered with trees and shrubs and flowers. In the midst of the island there was a high and beautiful tree, and below the tree was a deep well. The mariner was weak with hunger, and when he had searched in vain for fruit and failed to find it, for all the trees and shrubs were covered with flowers and dazzling gems, he approached the high and beautiful tree and said: 'May I find fruits on you lest I should perish with hunger.'

"When he had spoken these words, a strange wonder was seen by him. Suddenly there appeared on one of the branches of the tree ripe fruits of many varieties, which he immediately plucked and devoured to his heart's content. Before long he had eaten all the fruits which grew on the branch. Then he said: 'I would that there were grapes here also.' No sooner had he spoken thus than grapes appeared. He plucked them, and found they were of sweetness exceeding the sweetness of any grapes he had ever before tasted. 'T was thus he came to know that he had discovered the tree of the gods which yields whatever fruit is desired of it.

"The mariner was well pleased, and he said: Here will I dwell a time and fare well. Many feasts will I make off the bountiful wish-tree. I will also explore the wonderful island and gather together a store of dazzling gems, and when a ship comes near, I will hail it and return to my own land with great riches, and live for the rest of my days in joy and luxury.'

"The mariner sat down beside the deep well, and so clear and cool were its waters that he stooped to drink of them. He drank a deep draught, and found that the water refreshed body and soul, and imparted strength and joy to him such as he had never experienced before. Then a vision of beauty was unfolded before his eyes. As he gazed into the depths of the well he had glimpses of the radiant kingdom of Ocean. Then a fair sea-maid looked upwards with soft eyes and beckoned to him out of the blue-green depths. Immediately he followed her. He plunged into the well, and sank down and down until he reached the shining floor of Ocean beneath the island. He perceived with wonder that the wish-tree, which yielded whichever fruit was asked of it, rose from out of the depths, and had its roots in a ocean garden where the pebbles were little pearls and the soil was like fine gold dust.

"Boundless and beautiful was the country he found himself in. He beheld a golden palace and entered it, and found there, sitting on a golden throne, the Queen of Ocean. A splendor like a rainbow was behind the throne, and all around this splendor were gems that flashed like stars on a moonless night. The Queen had great beauty, and beautiful too were the ocean maids who waited upon her. When he saw the mariner she bade him to approach, ad she asked him: "Who are you, and where have you come from?"

"Said the mariner: 'I am one who has suffered shipwreck, and alone of all my companions do I remain alive. O lady of great beauty, I swam through the storm waves when my ship was broken by the tempest, and reached an island of many wonders. There I procured fruit from a tree which yields whatever is asked of it. I drink also from a well whose waters give great strength and happiness, and as I gazed into the well I saw one who beckoned to me, and I was drawn towards her I know not how or why.'

The Queen smiled upon him and spoke, saying: 'The face you saw was mine, and you come have here because I have power to draw you according to my will. Know that I am the Ocean Queen and the daughter of the king of all spirits. Know also that I have made a vow to take as my husband the first mortal who comes to my palace from the island of the wise-tree.'

The mariner was then given a throne to sit on, and the Ocean Queen became his bride. In great splendor he dwelt in the palace of the daughter of the King of all spirits, Princess Ratnamanjari.

Many days went past, and the mariner lived happily. It was a constant delight to him to explore the myriad wonders of the country of ocean, and he gathered together many gems and said: 'Now I have wealth beyond that which all the world of men contains. I am a prince who is mighty and powerful.

One day the Queen spoke to him and said: 'My well-loved husband, all that you see is yours to do with as it pleases your heart. But one thing is forbidden to you. That status of a beautiful Apsara (angel), which is of fine gold and is adorned with jewels, you must not touch. Forget not my words, nor ask of me why I have spoken thus.'

So much gold and so many gems were to be found for the seeking, that the mariner thought little of this restriction at first. But before long his eyes began to dwell on the statue, and he wondered greatly why he was forbidden even to touch it. Then it became his custom to sit before it, gazing with eyes full of wonder.

Said the Queen to him one evening: 'You see much beauty in the statue of the golden Apsara, but tomorrow I will take you to another palace which has greater wonders than can be seen here.'

Her words filled the mariner's heart with joy, but after she departed from him he wondered what would happen if he touched the forbidden statue. So he stretched forth his hand and laid it upon the right foot. Immediately the foot, which had the beauty of a lotus bloom, darted forward and went under his right arm and lifted him high. Speedily he rose through the deep as speedily, indeed, as one who, diving for pearls, darts downward to the sea floor. As he rose, the splendors of the golden palace faded and darkness pressed about him. All his strength then went from him, and when he rose from the sea and ascended through the air in moonless darkness, he become unconscious, and forgetfulness deep as death fell upon him.

When the mariner awoke from his swoon he found himself laying on the seashore of his own country. He was cold and wet and wretched. The rich robes in which he had been clad while he reigned in the kingdom of Ocean had vanished, and he wore instead a ragged woolen garment like a poor strolling player. He wandered about from city to city, and at length became one of a company of conjurors. Such, O mighty king, is my tale of the man who deserved punishment because he broke the law with knowledge,"

When the Rajah of the city of Silver Gates heard the wonderful story which the player related to him, his heart was well pleased, and he said: "Now ask of me whatever you wish, even if it be half of my treasure, and the same will be give to you."

Said the player: "O noble and mighty king, may your wisdom increase with knowledge. This mariner who broke the law was no other than he who now speaks to you. I have had great wealth and found no joy in it. Thy treasure therefore has no charm for me. But if you will grant the wish that is dearest to my heart, you will order that my son be set free so that we may wall depart in peace again."

Said the king: "You have spoken wisely and your wish will be granted. A son is a greater treasure to his father's heart than all the gold that the world can give."

Then was the lad set free, and the strolling players went on their way with happy hearts. And the king spoke to his son, the young prince, and said: "Henceforth you will obey the laws like other men until you sit in my place. You will still have whatever you desire, if what you asked for will increase knowledge which gives wisdom. The days of your childhood are ended. Now learn how to act as befits a good and great-hearted prince of the land."

A TRICKSTER PUNISHED

One day a jackal was hungry and roamed up and down a riverbank. He knew that food was plentiful on the other side, but was unable to cross over. He knew also that if he did cross over, he would have to return quickly, for there was a village near at hand and the people there would be sure to put him to death. After pondering awhile he devised a cunning scheme which would ensure his safety and a good meal also. He went in search of a camel, with whom he was friendly, and said to him: "You enjoy but poor fare in this place. I know where there is a field of sugarcane on the other side of the river, and if you will take me across on your back, I will lead you to it. There is some food for me there also—bones, and fragments of fish and dead birds of which I can make a hearty meal."

The camel said: "So be it. Jump on my back, and I'll swim across the river."

When they had reached the other side, the jackal led the camel to the field of sugarcane, and left him there. Then he himself went off to search for food. Before long he found a sufficient quantity of bones, and fragments of fish and dead birds to satisfy his hunger. Being as selfish as he was cunning, he then desired to return across the river without delay, although he was well aware that the camel was slow eater and would not be fully fed for some time. He sought to hasten his departure by raising an alarm. Running round the field of sugar-cane, he barked and howled as loudly as he could, so that the people of village might hear him. Then the people said: "There is a jackal in the sugar-field. He will begin to scratch holes in the ground; we had better drive him away."

When the villagers reached the field, carrying long staves in their hands, the jackal concealed himself. They did not, however, trouble to make search for him, for they saw the camel devouring the sugar-cane. This made them angry. They smote the camel with their staves, inflicting many painful wounds, and drove it along the river bank.

When the men turned away from the camel, the jackal run towards him and said: "We had better make escape at once, and cross over to the other side of the river. It is not safe for us to linger here."

Said the camel: "I quite agree with you. Just jump on to my back and I will swim again."

This was just what the jackal wanted, so he leapt on to the back of the camel, and licked his lips with satisfaction as his injured friend waded out into the water.

"You have been very badly wounded," said the jackal to the camel in a voice of mock sympathy.

"I have to thank you for that, my friend," the camel answered dryly. "You have behaved very badly."

"Oh, do not blame me," said the jackal. "I could not go to your assistance. I had to conceal myself from the cruel men, fearing they would put me to death. Had they struck me as they struck you, I should have been killed outright. It is fortunate you are so big and so strong. What a powerful animal you are!"

"If I am big and strong," the camel answered, "that is no reason why you should use me as you have done to suit your own purposes. How selfish and ungrateful you have been! When you had satisfied your hunger, you began to run round the field of sugar-cane, barking and howling, with the result that you alarmed the villagers and caused them to come and beat me with staves. I think you might have remained silent until I had enjoyed my meal."

"Well, I am sorry," said the jackal, "you think I am to blame in any way. I have always been accustomed to bark and howl with delight after feasting well.

By this time the camel had reached deep water. Then he spoke to the jackal and said: "We all have our habits, and now I must roll myself."

The jackal was immediately stricken with great fear, and said: " Please do not roll yourself here. If you do so, I shall be drowned and the blame will fall upon you."

"Well, I am sorry," the camel answered, "if you think I shall be to blame if any disaster happens to you. I have always been accustomed to roll myself after feasting."

As he spoke the camel rolled himself in the river, and the jackal fell from his back and was drowned.

When the camel reached the river bank, he shook himself and said: "We all have our habits, but the person who cultivates the habit of showing ingratitude to a benefactor who is greater and stronger than himself is likely to meet with the fate of the selfish jackal."

HOW THE MIGHTY SERVED THE WEAK

A trivial wrong may lead to many mishaps, and the plottings of a weak creature, who seeks revenge, involve the mighty in difficulties and compel their obedience. A small dark bird once obtained possession of three shells and counted himself rich, so he flew to the palace of great king and sang without ceasing: "I own three shells, O king; three shells I own."

At length the king grew weary of his song, and he spoke to one of his servants and said: "Go forth and seize the three shells, and chase away the tiresome dark bird." As the king commanded, so did the servant do. But the dark bird returned again to the palace and song persistently: "Rich have you grown with my treasure, O king; rich have you grown."

If the first song of the bird was wearisome, more wearisome still was the second. The king heard it with dismay, for it rang continuously in his ears, and he spoke to his servant who had robbed the bird, and said: "Restore the three shells to this chirper so that it may fly away." So the servant restored the shells, and then the bird, fearing to lose them again, spread his wings and departed from the king's palace. He flew straight to the city, and exchanged with a merchant the three shells for three dried peas. With them he departed and flew to the riverside. There a boat-builder was making a boat, and the bird perched upon it and sang: "I own three peas, O boat-builder; three peas I own." The men heard the bird, but took no heed of him because he was deeply engrossed in his labor.

In time the small dark bird began to devour the peas. When he swallowed the first he sang: "A pea have I eaten, O boat-builder; a pea have I eaten." The boat-builder heard but heeded not. Then the bird swallowed the second pea and sang: "Two peas have I eaten, O boat-builder; two peas have I eaten." To each individual his own affairs are most important, so the boat-builder went on with his work while the bird enjoyed its meal.

Then, as is chanced, the last of the peas rolled down into the boat, and fell into a crevice so that it became embedded at the keel. At this the bird became greatly excited, and flew round the boat-builder's head singing and wailing: "Restore my lost pea, O boat-builder; my lost pea restore."

The man stopped working, and, addressing the dark bird, said: "Foolish creature, how can I restore what you have lost? I cannot undo all I have done, and tear my boat plank from plank for the sake of a pea." So saying he resumed his labors, for he was anxious to complete them.

Sorrow filled the heart of the small dark bird, and he flew back to the palace of the king and sang: "O king, I have lost one of the peas which I purchased in the city. Commend the boat-builder, O you who see justice done, to restore it to me, as you commanded your servants to restore the shells."

Said the king: "Foolish Bird! The boat is of more account than your lost pea. Must the boat-builder suffer great loss so that you might be served?"

The bird flew to the queen, and sought to prevail upon her to entreat the king to command the boat-builder to restore the lost pea; but the queen said, "Foolish dark bird, fly away."

Said the bird: If you will not give me your aid, a swarm of wasps will come against you." But the queen only smiled at this empty threat.

Then the bird went to the wasps and asked them to attack the queen because she would not speak to the king, as was desired; but the wasps said, "Foolish bird, fly away."

Said the bird: "Fire will come against you if you will not do me this service." But the wasps took no heed of the bird.

Then the bird went to the fire and said: "O fire, go forth against the wasps, because the wasps will not attack the queen, because the queen will not prevail upon the king to order the boat-builder to restore my lost pea." But the fire tossed its burning locks with scorn and answered not.

Said the bird: "If you will not give me your aid, water will come against you and take your life."

So the bird next flew to a large pool and said: "O pool, rise and break thy banks, and go forth against the fire and quench it, because the fire will not attack the wasps, because the wasps will not attack the queen because the queen will not prevail upon the king to command the boat-builder to restore my pea."

The pool laughed scornfully, and said: "Foolish bird, fly away; do not weary me."

Said the bird: "O pool, if you will not do me this service the giant elephant, the king of all elephants, will come and drink up thy waters."

When he had uttered this threat, the bird flew of the king of Elephants, and said: "O King of Elephants, drink up the waters of the pool, because the pool will not quench of fire, because the fire will not attack the wasps, because the wasps will not attack the queen, because the queen will not prevail upon the king to command the boat-builder to restore my pea."

The king of Elephants snorted angrily and said: "Foolish bird, fly away; why should I serve you?"

Said the bird: "If you will not come to my aid, ants will enter your ears and begin to devour you."

Then the bird flew to the ants, and seized the King of Ants, and said: "If you will not order your armies to attack the elephant because he will not aid me, I will devour you and many of your kind."

Immediately the King of the Ants ordered his armies to go against the King of Elephants. And when the first ant entered the elephant's right ear and began to bite it, the elephant hastened to the pool and threatened to drink it up. The pool was deeply moved, and immediately burst its banks and flowed towards the fire. When the fire saw the waters coming, it leapt up and threatened the wasps, whereupon the wasps threatened the queen. The buzzing of the angry wasps alarmed the queen, and she hastened before the king and prevailed upon him to command the boat-builder to take his boat to pieces so that the lost pea might be recovered for the small dark bird. As the king commanded the boat-builder, so did he do.

Then the bird obtained the pea and devoured it, while the wasps returned to their own business, the fire became occupied with its own concerns, the pool shrank back into itself, the King of the Elephants returned to the forest, and the ants resumed their labors in their wonted manner. The king marveled that so trivial a matter as the loss of a pea should have upset the order of things and disturbed those with whom it had no concern. "Even a small dark bird," he said "must be listened to if there is to be peace in the kingdom."

THE CLEVEREST MAN IN THE WORLD

A rich nobleman had great skill with the bow and arrow, and was known as Sure Archer. Every day he bade his wife place a flower in hair, and stand at a distance of twenty paces from him in his garden. Then he shot an arrow and severed the stem, so that the bloom fell upon the ground. Each time he did this he spoke to his wife, saying: "Does there live in this world a cleverer man than I am?" And the woman was wont to answer: "Indeed, there is not in this world a cleverer man than you are."

Now, although Sure Archer's wife spoke thus, her heart was ever filled with dread when her husband commended her to stand with the flower in her hair, lest the arrow should be deflected and enter her head. Thinking of her peril, she slept restlessly by night, and during the day she wondered if she would be slain tomorrow. She grew thin and haggard and unhappy.

One day her brother visited her and asked: "Why do you look so ill and unhappy, O my sister?"

Said Sure Archer's wife: "Every morning my husband commands me to place a flower in my hair. Then he shoots an arrow and severs the stem. I am in constant dread lest the arrow should miss its mark some day and cause my death."

"Why does he do this?" the brother asked. Said his sister: "Because his skill is so great and it gives him delight. Each time he accomplishes this feat he asks me if there lives is this world a cleverer man than he is."

"What answer do you make?"

"I am wont to say: 'Indeed, no; there is not in this would a cleverer man than you are.'"

Said the brother: "When next your husband asks this question, answer him saying: 'Yes, there are cleverer men in this world than you are.' And if he asks further, 'How do you know?' make answer, 'My brother has said so.'"

As the brother adviser her, so did the woman speak. On the next morning, after her husband had severed with an arrow the stem of the flower which was in her hair and asked her if there was in world a cleverer man than he, she answered him saying: "Yes there are cleverer men in this world than you are."

"How do you know?" he asked with astonishment.

The woman answered: "My brother has said so."

"Your brother is great traveler," exclaimed Sure Archer, "and has seen all manner of men. If there exists in this world men who are cleverer than I am, I fain would meet with them. To-day I will set out on a journey to find if your brother has spoken truly."

Carrying his bow over his right shoulder, Sure Archer went forth alone and entered a deep forest. When night was drawing near he came to a mountain-side. There, sitting beside a well, he saw a man who had lit a fire and was preparing a meal.

Said the stranger: "Who are you and what do you seek?" Sure Archer answered: "My name is Sure Archer. I am searching for a cleverer man than I am. Who are you and what do you seek?"

Said the stranger: "My mane is Wrestler. I have never met my equal. I too am searching for a cleverer man than I am. Let us journey together, seeing we are on the same quest."

To this proposal Sure Archer agreed, and on the morrow the two men set forth and journeyed on ward through man, and they spoke to him, saying: "who are you and what do you seek?"

Said the man: " I am called Loud Roarer. I can roar louder than a lion or a Rakshasa (demon). I am searching for a man who is cleverer than I am.

Sure Archer said: "You need not search any longer. We are both as clever as you are. I am Sure Archer and my companion is Wrestler. Let us three travel together and discover if there can be found more accomplished men than we ourselves are."

Loud Roarer agreed to this, and next morning they all set forth together. After traveling a great distance they met a fourth man, and Sure Archer addressed him, asking: "Who are you and what do you seek?"

Said the man: "My name is Tumbler. I am a most accomplished gymnast. I can leap over a high tree and perform a somersault above it before I come down. Now I am searching for a cleverer man than I am."

"We are three highly accomplished men," said Sure Archer. " I am Sure Archer, my friend next me is Wrestler, and my other friend is Loud Roarer. Come with us and discover if there can be found in the would cleverer men than we are."

To this Tumbler agreed, and the four friends set out together next morning. They left the forest, and, as night was coming on, they reached a house which was situated on the slope a high mountain, overlooking a valley ran a broad, deep river, which entered the sea between masses of rock.

At the house door sat an old man, and when the four friends approached him he raised his head and spoke, saying: "Who are you and what do you seek?"

Sure Archer answered him, saying: "We are the most accomplished man in the world. I am Sure Archer, and my companions are named Wrestler, Loud Roarer and Tumbler. Together we are searching to find cleverer men than we are."

"You need not search any longer," the old man answered. "Clever indeed you all are. But I possess an accomplishment that none of you have. My name is Deep Thinker. Thought is greater than action, and the mind commands the body Your various accomplishment are of no use unless they are directed to some good purpose. Tarry here with me a little time, and I will be your counselor and guide."

The four travelers consented to do this, and they entered the house. There the wife of Deep Thinker provided them with food, and afterwards led them to the chamber in which she had made beds for them.

For a time the four friends talked together in whispers, and one said to the other: "Let us put this man, Deep Thinker, to test, for he has declared that he is more accomplished than any of us."

When Deep Thinker and his wife were fast asleep, the four men crept out of their chamber. Wrestler went down to the seaside, and carried a great boulder on his back which he placed before the door of the house. Meanwhile Sure Archer shot an arrow through a window, and it passed through the hair of Deep Thinker's wife and the pillow on which her head lay, but did not awaken her. Loud Roarer then uttered a mighty roar which resounded along the mountain-side, and Tumbler leapt over the house, performing a somersault above it; and so swiftly did he accomplish this feat that the noise he made in the air was like the flopping of eagles' wings.

Having each performed his part, the four companions crept through the window of their chamber and lay down. Exhausted by their feats, they at once fell into deep slumber.

The shout uttered by Loud Roarer awoke Deep Thinker and his wife. Said the woman: " A great Rakshasa has come near."

When she heard the rushing sound made by Tumbler as he leapt over the house, she said: "The Rakshasa in passing overhead." She attempted to raise her head, but found that her heir was firmly attached to the pillow. "Alas!" she cried, "the Rakshasa has thrust his hand into the chamber and seized me. Oh! help me, my husband, for he holds me fast."

Deep Thinker arose and procured a light. Then he perceived the arrow which bound his wife's hair to the pillow, and drew it out. She rose up trembling, and exclaimed: "What calamity has befallen us this night?"

Said Deep Thinker: "Have patience and fear not."

Together they left the chamber and went towards the door. Deep Thinker endeavored to open it, but was unable to do so because of the boulder which was outside.

"The Rakshasa prevents us from escaping," the woman wailed; but her husband said: "Have patience and fear not."

Together they entered the chamber in which the four companions lay asleep. Deep Thinker crept towards them. He looked at the bow and arrows of Sure Archer, and examined and hands and feet of Wrestler, touching then with his tongue. For a moment he gazed at Loud Roarer and Tumbler. Then he turned from the chamber and shut the door.

Returning to his own chamber with his wife, he crept through the window and went outside. He saw the boulder which Wrestler had carried from the seaside, and re-entered his house as he had left it, through the window. Then he assured his wife that all was well, and together they lay sown to sleep again.

Next morning Deep Thinker arose, and went and awoke the four companions. They sat up and rubbed their eyes.

Said Deep Thinker: "O Wrestler, a calamity has befallen this house. The door cannot be opened. Go out through the window and remove the boulder which was carried up from the seaside during the night. When you have done so, I will relate what I heard and all I know."

Wrester went through the window, and removed the boulder and opened the door.

Then Deep Thinker said: "The feat you performed is indeed remarkable, but I have not been deceived. You carried that boulder from the seaside and placed it before the door."

"How do you know that I did so?" asked Wrestler, who was greatly astonished.

Deep Thinker said: "I tasted the skin of your hands and feet while you lay asleep, and knew you had entered salt water, and I crept through the window of my chamber and saw the boulder."

Turning to Sure Archer, he spoke, saying: "You shot the arrow through the window in darkness and caused my wife's hair to be transfixed to the pillow. Your feat was also remarkable."

Said Sure Archer: "How do you know I did so?"

"When you arrived here last evening," Deep Thinker remarked, "I observed that you carried six arrows. When I crept into your chamber during the night I found that you had but five So I concluded that you had shot the arrow through the window."

To Loud Roarer he said: "You roared louder than a Rakshasa in the darkness;" and to Tumbler, "You leapt over the house with a rushing noise like the clapping of eagles' wings."

Said Sure Archer: "You have spoken truly, but how did you discover that it was Loud Roarer who roared, and Tumbler who leapt?"

Deep Thinker made answer: "I saw foam on the lips of Loud Roarer, and the muscles of Tumbler stood out like whipcords. After performing your feats, you all slumbered so deeply and helplessly that you were at my mercy, and I could have put you to death. I spared you because you were my friends. The exertions of the body bring sleep, but thought brings wakefulness. He who sleeps lightly and thinks deeply can achieve much. Wisdom is stronger than strength, and knowledge of more account than clever feats."

The four man said one to another: "This is indeed an accomplished man. He is more accomplished than we are so let us serve him a time."

That evening Deep Thinker spoke to the four men, saying: "Let us make merry and feast well," and they asked him, "Where will we procure food?"

Deep Thinker said: "Let Loud Roarer ascend the mountainside and utter a deep roar like a lion. Then the gazelles will rush hither. Sure Archer will shoot down the best-favored animal, and Wrestler will carry in to the house."

Said Tumbler: "What part will I take in this plan?"

Deep Thinker answered: "You time will come. Have patience and do as I command you."

Loud Roarer ascended the mountains, and when he had roared like a lion, a herd of gazelles leapt up and run towards the house.

Now it chanced that a Rakshasa came night at this time with evil intentions in his heart. When he saw the gazelles running down the mountain slope, he perceived that Deep Thinker desired to have one captured, so he joined the herd.

Before he did so, however, Sure Archer had shot down a gazelle, and the other fled away. Wrestler carried it towards the house.

Then Loud Roarer returned, and when he came to the house he spoke, saying: "Look yonder. The largest gazelle has not been slain. It stands on the spot where this one was slain."

Deep Thinker looked towards the gazelle and perceived that it was a Rakshasa, for its eyes flashed like fire. He spoke to Wrestler, saying: "Go towards that gazelle which has returned to the place where its companion fell, and carry it hither."

As Deep Thinker commanded, so did Wrestler do. He went towards the gazelle, and was greatly astonished when that animal charged him. Stepping aside, however, he seized it in his arms and carried it to Deep Thinker.

The Rakshasa Gazelle was greatly terrified, because he had never before met a man so strong as Wrestler.

Deep Thinker said: "This is not a gazelle but a Rakshasa. Now we can feast well. It is my custom to eat a Rakshasa every day, but I feared this day would pass without me finding one. So many have I devoured that they are growing scarce in my neighborhood."

When the Rakshasa heard these words, he immediately assumed his proper form and knelt before Deep Thinker, exclaiming: "Do not slay me, O Rakshasa devourer, and I will grant you whatever you ask of me. I will give you many gems if you will allow me to live."

Said Deep Thinker: "Must I be deprived of my Rakshasa food, which is dearer to me than many gems?"

The Rakshasa shed tears, and cried: "I will bring you larger and brighter gems than human eyes have ever beheld if you will grant my request."

Said Deep Thinker: "If I permit you to escape you will never return."

The Rakshasa answered: "I bind myself by the vow, which, if it is broken, will end my life, to return speedily with many gems."

Said Deep Thinker: "You ask of me a great favor indeed. I must sacrifice a meal to grant it. Nevertheless, I consent to allow you to depart. Hasten, therefore, and return here tomorrow with the gems of which you speak. If you do not return, I will go after you and devour not only yourself but also all your relations."

The Rakshasa then hastened away from the man whom he had intended to injure. Through the air he went with great swiftness, and as soon as he arrived home he entered the Rakshasa treasure chamber, which was beneath a mountain, and gathered together many gems. When he did so, he prepared to depart, but the Rakshasa king stopped him, saying: "Where are you going with these gems? Your duty is to guard them and not to carry them away."

Said the affrighted Rakshasa: "My life is in peril, and I must ransom it with the precious stones. A company of fierce beings who resemble men, and are yet greater than men, dwell on a mountain-side near a river mouth. They are eaters of Rakshasas, and have threatened to devour me and all my family if I did not procure treasure for them."

The Rakshasa king wondered to hear these words. "You may carry the gems to these men like beings, "he said, "but only on condition that you will prevail upon them to come here with you when you return. I will summon all my subjects to assemble together and discuss this matter."

Said the affrighted Rakshasa: "Alas! Whichever way I turn death confronts me. If I remain here, the fierce people will follow me and catch me and eat me up, and if I do not bring them before the king, my kinsfolk will tear me to pieces."

He then took his departure, and hastened with the gems to Deep Thinker, who frowned, saying: "Why have you not come sooner? Three days have passed since I commanded you to bring this treasure. I was just about to go after you."

Said the Rakshasa: "My king detained me, and has commanded that I should entreat you and your companion to visit him. A great assembly of Rakshasas is to be held tomorrow to consider what should be done regarding such fierce people as you are."

"I will go with you," answered Deep Thinker, "and my friends will go also, but you must carry us all."

Said the Rakshasa: "Deeply grateful am I to you. Consider me your faithful slave. I will carry you all to the great assembly."

Broad was the back of the Rakshasa and his strength was great. He carried Deep thinker, Sure Archer, Wrestler, Loud Roarer, and Tumbler through the air, traveling swiftly as the wing. All day he went onward and all night. When the next morning had dawned, he drew near to a forest clearing in which the Rakshasas were beginning to assemble.

Said Deep Thinker: "Set us together on a branch of that high tree."

The Rakshasa did as he was commanded. He set the five companions on the tree branch and they set there, gazing down upon the assembly. In a high throne sat the Rakshasa king. He had a body like a bull and a mouth like a tiger. Terrible was he to look upon. Round him sat hundreds of blood-thirsty rakshasas, growling like hungry lions and chattering like apes.

The Rakshasa who had carried Deep Thinker and his companions to the assembly approached his king, who spoke, saying: "Where are the fierce manlike creatures whom you promised to bring here?"

"They are in that tree," was the answer.

All the Rakshasas looked towards the tree, and Deep Thinker said to Loud Roarer: "Roar now." As he commanded, so did his companion. He roared so loud that all the Rakshasas trembled.

The Rakshasa king looked at the men in silence for a time. Then the said: "Come down."

Said Deep Thinker to Tumbler: "Leap down and leap back."

No sooner had he spoken thus, than Tumbler leapt to the ground. Many clawlike hands were stretched forth to seize him, but he leapt again high in the air towards the king, over whose head he performed a somersault. Then he came to the ground behind that monarch, overturning six Rakshasas as he did so. Quick as lightning, he at once leapt again and returned to the tree. As he did so, Loud Roarer, drawing a deep breath, roared louder and longer than before. All the Rakshasas were terrified except the king, who said: "They roar and they leap, but what injury can they do?"

Deep Thinker heard the words, and he spoke to Sure Archer, saying: "Shoot, but do not slay him."

Sure Archer at once drew his bow and shot an arrow which pierced the right ear of the Rakshasa king, and remained stuck fast in it.

The fierce monster roared with fear, and cried out: "I will tear up the tree by its roots and shake off these fierce creatures and devour them."

As he spoke, the branch of the tree snapped with the weight of the five companions, and they fell to the ground.

Said Deep Thinker: "Now let each man display his skill or we shall all perish."

Loud Roarer uttered a still roar than before, Tumbler leapt into the air, performing double somersaults, Sure Archer shot many arrows, and Wrestler sprang at the king. If the Rakshasa king was strong, the Wrestler was stronger, for he overthrew the monster and broke his right arm.

Then Deep Thinker cried out: "Slay the Rakshasa king, and we will devour him with the others who are wounded with arrows."

"Spare me, spare me," moaned the Rakshasa king, "and I will give you many gems."

All his subject fled away and concealed themselves, some shrieking with the pain of their arrow wounds, and other in abject fear.

Deep Thinker spoke to the Rakshasa king, and said: "We will spare you life if you will promise to do as we command you."

Said the Rakshasa: "I will obey you willingly if you spare my life."

"Then," Deep Thinker said, "bid the Rakshasa who took us thither to return with us again Being great rulers, we must be carried. Besides, it is a law recognized everywhere that each portion of ground which our feet trend upon becomes part of our domains."

Said the Rakshasa king: "Your command will be obeyed."

"As for the treasure, "said Deep Thinker, "we need much of it, but do you think that we who are accustomed to be served will take it with us? You must send it to our home on the mountain slope beside the river mouth. See that five Rakshasas are heavily burdened with gems, and that they deliver them to us in two days."

Said the Rakshasa king: "Your command will be obeyed."

"If we find it necessary to return," Deep Thinker said, "we will devour you and all your subjects."

Sitting on the back of their Rakshasa servant, the five companions returned to the house on the mountain-side. They waited there for two days. Then five Rakshasas came, carrying much treasure. They came quickly, and when they had unburdened themselves of gems, were glad to return quickly.

Said Deep Thinker: "Now let us divide our treasure into equal parts, and each go his own way."

This they did, but they parted one from another with regret.

Said Sure Archer: "O Deep Thinker, what you said when first we met is indeed true. Thought is greater than action. Our accomplishments are of no use unless they are directed to some good purpose. You have proved yourself a mighty counselor and guide. Indeed, you are the cleverest man in the world."

The other spoke likewise; and Deep Thinker answered: "Boast not of your accomplishment, nor let them make you vain. Each many fulfils his part in this life, and he who is weak of limbs is as necessary as he who is strong. One rules and many serve, and those who serve do so by virtue of their merits. Despise not your fellows, but seek to discover wherein lies the strength of those who differ from you. A man cannot live alone, or act alone. A king cannot rule who has no subjects, and subjects cannot direct their energies rightlt unless they are guided by a wise ruler. I bid you all farewell, and may you live happily until the appointed time when you are judged according to your deeds and your knowledge."

Then the five companions parted and went their various ways. Sure Archer returned home with his share of the treasure, and his wife welcomed him with love. "I have traveled far," he said, "and learned much. All these gems I have brought back for you to keep. Your brother spoke truly. In this world there are many men who are cleverer than I am, but the cleverest of all is Deep Thinker. But for Deep Thinker, Wrestler, Loud Roarer, and Tumbler, I would not have obtained this treasure. Never again will I make boast of my skill with the bow. Let us live happily until death calls us."

For the rest of their days Sure Archer and his wife lived happily, and they were blessed with many children. When the children grew to years of wisdom, Sure Archer spoke often to them, saying: " Love one another while life endures. Let each one discover the merits of each other and admire them, and be humble of heart, nor boast, nor be vain."

PERILS OF WEALTH

A poor man fell heir to a large fortune and said: "Now I can have everything my heart desires. No longer need I fear starvation. It is a blessed thing to have great wealth. Oh! I shall hoard it up and use it carefully."

A Brahman who heard these words remarked: "That was what the greedy jackal said, but he died because he had miser's spirit."

"How did that come about?" asked the man.

"Listen to me," the Brahman said, "and I will tell you the story." And this was the story which the Brahman told:

There was a great hunter who lived in a town called Prosperity. One day he said: "I must obtain some venison. So he seized his bow and arrows and went out into the forest. Before long he brought down a fine deer. Being very strong, he threw the deer across his shoulders and turned towards his home.

He had not gone far when a great wild boar came dashing through the forest, attracted by the smell of blood. No sooner did hunter observe it than he threw down the deer, and, bending his bow, shot an arrow. The boar was wounded, but the pain it suffered made it fiercer than ever. With a loud roar it charged the huntsman just as he fixed another arrow in his bow, and, throwing him down, tore him open with its tusks. Then it fell dead beside him, crushing a passing snake as it fell.

Not long after a jackal came near, searching for food. When he perceived the bodies of the hunter, the deer, the boar, and the snake, he chuckled in great glee, and said: "Today I have good fortune indeed. Hear is a fine feast laying ready for me. Indeed, there is food to last me for several weeks. This man will keep me eating for a month, the deer will provide rich meals for another month, and then I shall have the boar. This snake will serve me for to-morrow. As I do not feel very hungry today, I shall just have a bite of the gut at the end of the bow."

The jackal then closed his teeth over the gut, and when he gave but a single tug, the bow-string was unloosed from the dead man's finger, and out sprang the arrow, which pierced the heart of the greedy animal. The jackal fell back dead beside the great store of food it had found.

"Such is my story," said the Brahman to the poor man who had suddenly grown rich. "The lesson it teaches is obvious."

"What is it?" asked the man.

"Great wealth is difficult to handle," the Brahman answered. "Besides, one may be frugal and yet not be a miser.'

THE MOUSE WHO BECAME A TIGER

A king who lived in olden times was famed far and wide as a just and generous ruler. He protected the weak against the strong, and caused the robber-bands among the mountain to respect the laws. Peace prevailed everywhere throughout the kingdom. "Happy is the ruler", he was wont to say, "who is loved by his subjects because he does what is right and hates the wrong."

When the king grew old he spoke to his son: "If you desire to follow my example and live peacefully all your days, see that you choose men of great merit to administer the laws."

He had hardly spoken thus when a messenger arrived at the palace with alarming tidings. "Alas! Your Majesty," he said, "a rebellion has broken out among the mountain tribes."

Said the king: "Must blood be shed so that lawless men may be convinced of their folly? My heart is filled with sorrow to think of it. But there is no need for alarm, for my faithful governor Jivaka will deal with these rebels and assert my authority in no uncertain manner."

The messenger bowed his head and answered: "The rising in more serious than your Majesty realizes, for Jivaka, whom you have favored and trusted, and raised from humble rank to govern the mountain tribes, is himself the leader of revolt. He aspires to dethrone you and rule over the kingdom.

Said the king: "Let a strong army be sent against him, and may his punishment be as great as is his folly."

Then a strong army was dispatched towards the mountains to capture the rebel governor and scatter his forces.

Once again the Rajah spoke to his son regarding the manner

in which he should rule, and said: "My years are many and my experience ripe. Yet I have found that wise and just although my laws may be, they are set at naught by an unfaithful administrator. I trusted Jivaka as if he were my own son. On him I conferred honors, but his heart knows not what gratitude is. Have the gods stricken him with madness that he should lift his hand against me, his benefactor?"

Said the chief queeen: "Has lord never heard the story of the Brahman and the mouse?"

"If the story will help me to understand the treachery of Jivaka," the Rajah said, "relate it to me."

Said the chief queen: "The story teaches that he who gives authority to an ungrateful man lays bare his breast of the dagger. When the mouse become a tiger he sought to slay his benefactor."

"How came that about?" asked the king.

"Listen and I will tell you," the chief Rani said. And this was the tale she related to the king:

A Brahman who lived in a deep forest had achieved great power by reason of the austerities which he practsed. One day he was sitting at the door of his hermitage when a crow, which was flying overhead, let fall from its beak a small field mouse. The little animal ran towards the Brahman for protection, and he gave it food to eat.

"Allow me to dwell here," entreated the mouse. "I can find no protection in my home, for the crow has devoured my parents, and if I return he will certainly devour me also."

Said the Brahman: "So be it. Here you may dwell without fear. I will protect you against your enemies."

The mouse shared the Brahman's meals, and soon began to grow strong and bold. In time it ventured forth from the hermitage, feeling confident that none of its enemies would dare approach it. But one evening a cat came near, and beholding the mouse, at once gave chase, saying: "The mouse is fat and full of rich blood. My stomach yearns for it."

The Brahman observed that the mouse was in danger of being caught before it reached the hermitage, and immediately transformed it into a large cat which fought and drove away the other.

Said the mouse: "Now I have no fear of cat enemies, for you, my protector, have made me the strongest cat in the world."

For a time the mouse-cat lived happily. Then the dogs came to worry it. One evening the Brahman saw his favorite being chased by a large black dog, and he immediately transformed it into a larger dog which fought and drove away the other.

Said the mouse: "Now I have no fear of dog enemies, for you, my protector, have made me the strongest dog in the world."

As it happened, however, the tigers grew jealous of the mouse-dog, and said: "if this strong dog grows stronger, it will come against our young ones. Let us therefore put it to death at the first opportunity."

One evening the Brahman saw the mouse-dog running towards the hermitage, pursued by a fierce tiger and he immediately transformed his favorite into a fiercer tiger, which fought and drove away the other.

Said the mouse: "Now I have grown mighty indeed. O my protector, how can I thank you? You have shown me great favors. I may roam anywhere now without fear. As the hermitage is too small for me, I must dwell in the jungle."

The Brahman said: "Come here often, for my heart has been moved towards you. Although others may fear you, remember that to me you will ever be a little pet mouse."

The people who dwelt near the jungle were at first afraid of the mighty tiger which they saw from time to time wandering about, but the Brahman comforted them by relating all that had taken place, and said: "Have no fear, for it is only my little pet mouse whom I have transformed so that none of its enemies may attack it."

So it came about that the people were no longer afraid. When they saw the mighty animal in the jungle they exclaimed: "Although the tiger is lordly to look upon, and so large and mighty, it is just a mouse after all, which the Brahman has transformed."

The mouse tiger heard these mocking words and felt angry. Before long it said: "This state of matters must come to an end. I will never be respected either by men or wild animals so long as the Brahman remains alive, for he will always remind every one of my humble origins. I must therefore slay him and have myself proclaimed the king of this jungle."

That night the tiger crept towards the hermitage to fall upon its benefactor. But the Brahman had knowledge of its purpose, and at once transformed the ungrateful animal into its mouse shape again. When this happened it ran away, and no sooner had morning dawned than a crow seized it and devoured it.

The people came to know of what had happened, and they said: "Because the mighty tiger had the mind of a mouse, it brought about its own destruction. Vanity and ingratitude go hand in hand, and treachery follows in their steps."

When the king heard this story he bowed his head, and spoke to his son, saying: "This Jivaka will meet the fate of the mouse when the crows of my army reach the mountains. Be warned by my shortcomings, and know that good laws are of no avail unless they are administered by good men."

A GREEDY HERON

A large crab was crawling along the bottom of a pool when suddenly he came upon a heron which was standing on one leg
and looking very melancholy.

"Why are you so sad, my friend?" the crab asked.

"Have you not heard the news?" remarked the heron, looking surprised.

Now the crab was a great gossip, and immediately squatted
down to engage in a chat, for fresh news was as sweet to him as a
meal.

"I have heard nothing," he said. "Please tell me at once everything you know."

Said the heron: "Perhaps you have observed that I am fond
of feeding. I have a special liking for fish."

"That has not escaped my observation," the crab commented.

"You can understand, therefore," continued the heron, "how
I feel when I think of what the fishermen intend to do."

"And what is their intention?" asked the crab.

"I am told on good authority," the heron lamented, " that
they have resolved to spread a net and capture every fish in this
populous pool. What a great shame that will be! I do not mind so
much for my self, because I can go to some other pool, but I cannot
help feeling for the fish. My heart is filled with sorrow for them.
What have they done to deserve such treatment?"

"This is terrible news indeed," exclaimed the crab. "I must
inform the fish."

Now some of the fish overheard what the heron had said,
and those who did not overhear were informed by the crab.

Said the fish, one to another: "What is to be done? We are quite helpless. Had we not better consult the heron who has been good enough to inform us of this approaching calamity, which affects him as much as it does ourselves? Enemies become friends when threatened by a common danger."

So they sent the crab to speak with the heron and the crab said to that melancholy-looking bird: "Dear fellow-creature, the fish desire to know what they should do to save themselves from destruction by the heron: "So far as I can see, there is only one means of escape, and that is to leave the pool. As the fish cannot do this of their own accord, I am willing to carry them to another pool, where they will have no need to fear the fishermen."

When the fish were informed of this proposal, they exclaimed, "So be it," and at once swam in a body to the corner of the pool in which the heron stood.

One by one the cunning bird lifted the fish from the water and walked away. He did not, however, go another pool, but swallowed each fish in turn, standing below a tree, where he ejected the bones. In this manner he devoured them all.

When there was not a single fish left in the pool, the crab felt very lonely, and he asked the heron to remove him also. Now the heron, who was a great glutton, never seemed to be satisfied, and had a great desire to taste the tender flesh of the crab. So he lifted him gently and walked towards the tree. But the crab kept his eyes wide open, and when he saw the heap of fish bones on the ground, he suddenly realized the fate that was in store for him. He resolved to make a fight for life. So he stretched out his great toes and seized the heron by the throat. A fierce struggle ensued. The bird endeavored to throw down the crab, but the crab held on firmly until he had torn open the crane's neck and killed him. Thus it came about that the cunning bird perished because it was a deceiver.

Said the crab: "The greatest rascal will meet his match some day."

Then he crawled back to the pool, and seeing it was once again being filled with fish, said: "How much the heron has missed because of its greed! He who fares well on fish should not attempt to swallow crabs."

THE BLUE JACKAL

A young jackal, who had no special accomplishments, was so exceedingly vain that he desired to become king of all the wild beasts. One day he walked out of the family den with his head uplifted, and his mother called after him, saying: "Where are you going?"

Said the young jackal: "I am ambitious and desire to seek fame and fortune."

"My advice to you," his mother remarked, "is to remain a little longer here and learn wisdom. Jackals never acquire either fame or fortune, but they can live quite happily so long as they follow the ways of their kind." Said the young jackal: "I was born to become great, and will not rest content until I have grown mighty and powerful."

"Alas!" exclaimed the mother jackal, "what can a parent do when good advice is scorned by her offspring?"

The young jackal wandered away through a forest, and at length came to the work place of a dyer. There he fell into a vat, and when he crept out he discovered that his hair had all been dyed blue.

"How fortunate!" he exclaimed. "Really, I am the child of luck. I do not believe that in all the world there is another blue jackal."

He went on his way, and met some jackals who regarded him with fear and wonder. "This is a holy animal," they said.

The young jackal was quite flattered, and said: "You humble jackals, listen to me. My name is Shatag, and Indra, the king of gods has elevated me to be the king of the forest."

When startled jackals heard this, they ran hither and thither and told every animal they met that Indra had chosen a new king, who was to rule over all the wild beasts.

The lions and lionesses were much concerned by the news, and hastened to inform the lion king. That mighty animal, whose mane was long and shaggy, said: "Hasten and see what manner of wild beast has been sent here by Indra." As he commanded, so did the lions and lionesses do. They hastened towards the blue jackal and gazed upon him with wonder. The elephants and the tiger had gathered to honor the new ruler, and the blue jackal sat on the back of the highest bull elephant in the forest. When this was told to the lion king, he was greatly troubled.

All the wild beasts were summoned to do homage before the blue jackal, and he said: "Hasten to the den of my mother and bid her come here without delay, so that she may watch my triumph."

The shift-footed jackal did as he was commanded. He ran towards the den of the mother jackal and delivered the message.

Said the mother: "How are the wild beasts arranged at my son's court?"

The messenger, answering her, said: "Your son, the blue jackal, is seated on the back of the bull elephant. Around him is a ring of elephants. The next ring is formed by tigers, and the third ring by lions. Jackals are ranged round in an outer ring."

Said the mother jackal: "So my son is isolated from his kind. The proper order of things is disturbed."

The messenger jackal said: "He bids you to attend his court."

Said the mother Jackal: "It is not my custom to leave my den except when I desire to eat food or drink refreshing water. I am safe here. My son will also remain safe until he begins to howl like any other jackal."

The messenger returned to the court of the blue jackal and addressed his fellows, saying: "The blue king is just a common jackal like ourselves. I have seen his mother and she refuses to come here, preferring to stay in her den, where she feels safe."

A wise old jackal said: "if the king is really a jackal, he is an imposter. Let us test him by howling."

Now it is a belief among jackals that they must all howl with their fellows, and that the jackal which remains silent will lose its hair.

When the jackals began to howl, the blue king said to himself: "If I do not answer them, my hair will fall off and the wild beasts will cease to do me homage." So he opened his mouth and howled aloud.

The great elephant heard him and said: "Why, the blue king who sits on my back is just a common jackal. Who could mistake his voice? We have all been deceived."

When he had spoken thus, he shook the impostor from his back, and stamped on him. Thus did the vain jackal perish suddenly in the height of his triumph.

The messenger jackal ran swiftly to the den of the mother jackal, and told her what had taken place. Tears fell from her eyes, but she did not express any astonishment. Addressing her other children, she said: "In a time a danger it is best to be among one's own friends. A jackal may pretend to greatness by wearing a blue coat, but he will never deceive other beasts when he begins to howl."

IMPORTANCE OF GOOD ADVICE

There was once a talkative tortoise. He lived beside the pool of the Blue Lotus, and was an intimate friend of a family of wild geese. He was in the habit of relating to them all the gossip of the neighborhood, and they regarded him as a most entertaining companion, although they couldn't help acknowledging that he talked too much. The mother goose was afraid sometimes that he would attract their enemies to the pool, so loud and constant a chatter did he keep up.

One evening the tortoise arrived home looking very doleful. He was asked what had gone wrong, and the geese marveled greatly to see tears falling from his eyes. "My news is indeed sorrowful," the tortoise said. "I have been listening to the conversation of some fishermen who planned among themselves to visit the pool tomorrow morning, and catch all the fish and tortoises and geese. Alas!" he moaned, "what am I to do?"

Said geese: "Are you quite sure there is any danger of calamity?"

"I am only too certain," the tortoise assured them, "and am as anxious to avoid it as the fish called 'No-Time-To-Wait' and 'Nimble-in-Danger'. These two escaped the fishermen, but 'What-must-be-must-be' was caught in the net."

"Tell us about them," the geese entreated.

Said the tortoise: "The three fish dwelt in a pool just like this one and came to know that fishermen were intending to spread a net for them. The fish called 'No-Time-To-Wait' exclaimed: 'I shall swim to another pool at once.' No sooner did he say so than he took his departure. 'Nimble-in-Danger' said: 'There is no reason why one should leave here unless he is forced to.' The third fish,

'What-must-be-must-be', shook his head and muttered: 'What must not be, must not be and what must be, must be. There is no medicine for a sorrowful heart like a comforting thought." He went on feeding.

"In the morning the fishermen came and cast their net in the pool. Both fish were caught, but Nimble-in-Danger lay pretending to be dead until the net was lifted out of the water; then he leapt back into the pool again. Such a feat was impossible for What-must-be-must-be, who resigned himself to his sorrowful condition and allowed himself to be seized. The fishermen caught and ate him. I have no desire to share his fate," concluded the tortoise. "Indeed, it is my desire to act like No-Time-to-Wait. But how can we do so is a problem which baffles me."

Said the elder goose: "The way to escape is to go away somewhere, but unfortunately you are unable to go very fast. As for ourselves, we can fly away."

"Why not take me with you?" tortoise asked. " I would go much faster through the air than along the ground."

The geese laughed. "You cannot come with us," they declared, "because you are unable to fly."

Said the tortoise: "One may make good his defects by obtaining the assistance of friends. I suggest that I should grasp a stick in my mouth, and that two of you should hold it at either end and convey me to a place of safety."

The elder goose nodded and smiled. "The proposal," he declared, "is an excellent one, but remember that it is one thing to make wise plans and another thing to carry them out."

"I am quite prepared to do my part," said the tortoise. "I will seize the stick in my mouth and hang on to it."

"But what if you should desire to talk, as is your custom?" the elder goose suggested. "That is the danger. If you opened your mouth as we fly through the air, you would fall down and be killed."

Said the tortoise: "Do you think I am such a fool as to open my mouth you are carrying me? No, no. Come, let us be going. Here is an excellent stick."

"There are times," the elder goose remarked, "when silence is best."

Two geese then grasped in their beaks the stick which the tortoise had seized, and rose high in the air. As they flew onward they passed over a village, and the people came out and looked up with astonishment and amusement.

"There goes a flying tortoise," laughed one man.

"He will fall soon," another jeered; "then we shall eat him."

The tortoise heard what they said and felt very angry. He disliked being mocked at.

A third man cried: "Gather sticks and light a fire. We shall cook and eat that tortoise at once."

The tortoise could keep silence no longer. "Eat me? — Eat ashes," he cried.

No sooner did he open his mouth than he lost hold of the stick and fell to the ground. The villagers laughed, and seized him at once.

Said the elder goose: "There he goes. Has it not been well said that he who neglects good advice is sure to meet with calamity.

THE WISE APE

An old ape once lived on the edge of forest, and the tree he was wont to frequent was old also. He was famed far and wide for his wisdom, and when wild animal disagreed regarding any matter, they were accustomed to visit him so that he might judge between them. Many stories are told regarding this wise ape, and one of these is as follows:

A Brahman once entered a village near the forest and saw a strong cage in which a tiger was imprisoned. This fierce animal was a man-enter who had been caught in a snare. At first the villagers desired to put him to death; but when they were told by a sage that their enemy had in his former life been a greedy and cruel moneylender of ill repute, they resolved to keep him confined lest he should assume a still more terrible form, or perhaps become once again a human being who loved nothing better than to be a persecutor of his kind.

When the Brahman looked at the tiger, he perceived that there were tears in his eyes, so he spoke with sympathy, saying: "What ails you, O fellow-creature?"

Said the tiger: "You are a good and holy man, and you heart is full of pity. Help me in my distress. I am parched with thirst. Open the door of my cage so that I may go down to the river and drink my fill."

"If I release you," the Brahman answered, "you will devour me. And even if you did not do so, the villagers would be angry with me. They have no desire that you should regain your freedom."

Said the tiger: "O pious one, I vow not to harm you. When I have satisfied my thirst, I will return to my cage again."

The Brahman pitied the tiger, and, opening the door of the cage, allowed him to leap forth.

Said the tiger: "Now I will devour you. I can drink water afterwards. For many days I have not obtained a proper meal."

"I bind you to observe your vow to this extent," the Brahman answered: "that you will not devour me until we have stated our pleas before seven judges."

Said the tiger: "So be it. Let us have the opinions of the judges."

First of all they went before the green parrot. The Brahman spoke at length, and then the tiger stated his views.

Said the green parrot: "I have lived among men and can speak their language. My master was a rich merchant, and when I was in full plumage he admired me greatly. I amused him with my clever sayings, but no sooner did I begin to grow old and ugly than he chased me away to find my own food. As he had clipped my wings, I could not fly far, and now I lead a miserable existence. My kins-folk will not associate with me because I have assumed so many foreign manners, and human being despise me because I can no longer amuse them. Men are fickle and cruel. Therefore, O tiger, devour the Brahman as is your desire."

The tiger was ready to devour the Brahman without further delay, but the pious and holy one said: "We must hear the judgments of the other six animals yet."

Next they when before the ass. When that animal heard that the Brahman and the tiger had to say, he spoke as follows: "I was once strong and nimble. My master laid great burdens upon my back, and forced me to carry them long distances. He was never grateful for my assistance, and not only did he grudge me food, but constantly struck me with a stave. Now that I have grown stiff and old, he treats me more cruelly then ever. He has made my daughter his slave, and if I venture to approach her stable he throws stones at me, or else lets loose the dogs to torment and drive me away. Men are devoid of pity. Therefore show no pity to the Brahman, O tiger, but devour him forthwith."

Said the tiger: "Wisely have you spoken, O ass. As you advise so will I do."

But the Brahman interposed, saying: "We have heard but two judgments. Let us now go before the camel."

To the camel they went, saying: "We desire you to hear our pleas and deliver judgment."

Said the camel: "Very well. But you must both be brief, for I have just begun to feed."

The Brahman and the tiger spoke briefly one after the other, and the camel said: "The case is very simple, and I have no hesitation in giving my judgment. Like the tiger, I have endured suffering at the hands of mankind. Why do I limp and eat slowly? Because I have had dealings with human being. He says he wants justice. A human being is never just to wild or tame animals. Therefore he does not deserve to be treated justly. Eat the Brahman, O tiger."

The tiger was ready to do so, But the Brahman said: "Now let us go before the jackal."

To the jackal both spoke at length, and the judgment he gave was this: "Were it not for human beings, all beasts of prey would lead happy lives. Men are our natural enemies. Therefore the tiger should deal with the Brahman as he would with any other enemy." This was a pleasing judgment to the tiger.

Next they visited the alligator, who said: "Like the tiger, I prefer human flesh to any other. But men give no consideration to our needs. Although there are more men than alligators, we can never get our rightful share of food. What we do get is obtained by guile. The tiger has acted with guile by necessity. Therefore let the tiger eat this man. He can get no guarantee that a substitute will be provided."

The tiger roared approval and was about to leap on the Brahman, but the wise man said: "Be patient; I have not yet exhausted the resources of the law. Now I appeal to the eagle."

As he spoke, an eagle flew round in circles above them and consented to hear their pleas. He did not seem to pay much attention to what was said, and without hesitation gave his judgment, which he delivered thus: "The tiger has suffered. Every creature who is brought into touch with human being endures suffering. See how they deal with me. They shoot arrows against me, and climb the cliffs to rob my nest and kill my young ones. It is the duty of all wild animals to deal wit man in the peculiar human way. The treacherous must be punished with treachery. Let the tiger eat this man.

Said the tiger: "My patience is exhausted, O Brahman. Six judges have delivered judgment against you. Therefore, prepare to die."

The Brahman made answer: "Be not so impatient. One judge remains yet to be heard."

"Who is he?" asked the tiger.

"The last judge," the Brahman said, "is the wish ape. He dwells not far from here. I must abide by his final judgment."

"My patience is almost exhausted," growled the tiger, "but, having gone to law, one must follow the process laid down and drag out his dispute to the bitter end."

So the tiger and the Brahman went before the ape, and each stated his case very clearly and strongly.

Said the ape: "This is a most interesting dispute. Both of you have spoken well, and it is now time for me to give my judgment. The case is not so simple as it appears on the surface. There is much to be said for the Brahman's plea, and there is much to be said for the tiger's. To set my mind at rest, I must first of all visit the place where the dispute arose. Where is the cage that has been spoken of?"

Said the tiger: "O wise judge, I will lead you to the cage in which the cruel villagers kept me a prisoner without giving me sufficient food and drink." Then the ape accompanied the tiger and the Brahman to the cage. When he reached it, he said: "So this is the cage. Now, O Brahman, where were you standing when you first spoke to the tiger?"

Said the Brahman, walking forward to the right-hand corner of the cage: "I stood here."

"Is that correct, O tiger?" the ape asked.

"Quite correct," answered the tiger.

"Now," continued the ape, "I wish to know where you were standing, O tiger."

The tiger at once leapt into the cage and stood facing the Brahman.

"Is that correct, O Brahman?" asked the ape

"Quite correct," was the answer.

"So for so good," the ape commented. "There is another point which I should like to have made clear. It is this. Was the cage open or shut when the Brahman first spoke to the tiger?"

"It was shut," the tiger said.

"Why was I not told this before?" asked the ape, speaking impatiently. "How can I be expected to give judgment in a case unless I am acquainted with all the facts? If the cage was shut to begin with, let it be shut now."

The Brahman at once closed the door of the cage bolted it.

"The case looks simpler now," remarked the wish ape. "I

have only one other question to ask of you both. Now tell me, did the tiger ask to be let out because he was hungry, or because he was thirsty?"

"Because he was thirsty," the Brahman answered.

"I was both hungry and thirsty," growled the tiger.

"Ah! You are not agreed on this point," the ape said. "The evidence is at variance. The Brahman's case is that the tiger wanted to drink water, and that he opened the door of the cage so that the tiger might hasten to the river. On the other hand, the tiger declares he was hungry as well as thirsty. If he was let out to appease his hunger in the first place, it is evident he expected to eat the Brahman. There can be no doubt about that: the tiger's subsequent actions prove it clearly. But there is no proof that the Brahman consented to be eaten. His consent, I think was necessary, but it was not obtained. I must therefore dismiss the case. If the tiger holds that he has a right to devour the Brahman, let him now take the necessary step of asking the Brahman's consent. If the Brahman gives it, there will be no need to go to law again. Such is my judgment. I bid you both good day, and can only add that it has given me much pleasure to deal with this case, which has raised some interesting points in law.

Having spoken thus, the ape turned away; and the Brahman addressed the tiger saying: "I took pity on you because I believed you were tortured by thirst. I trusted you and opened the door of the cage. You need not ask me to do so again. You are both evil-hearted and ungrateful. Therefore I will take my departure and leave you to endure both hunger and thirst."

The tiger lashed his tail and growled and snarled. But the Brahman went on his way, rejoicing that there was justice in the land. "But for the law," he said, "and especially when it is administered by a just judge, good men would never find protection against the claims of tigers."

STORY OF THE STAR MAIDENS

I n days of long ago three star maidens looked down upon the
earth with loving eyes, and their hearts were filled with desire to
visit it. Seeing a lotus-fringed pool in the midst of a deep forest,
they said: "Gladly would we bathe in it." But they knew not how
they could descend to this forest pool, and all night long they gazed
down with wonder and yearning.

On the next night they peered at the pool again. Said the
elder star maiden: "It is more beautiful than ever. Would I could
reach it." The others spoke in the same manner." As it happened,
their words were heard by the moon lady, who loved a high mountain, and was wont to wander over its wooded slopes. She spoke
to the star maidens and said: " If you would fain reach the forest
pool, climb down the web of the King of Spiders, which reaches
from the heavens to the earth."

The King of spiders was sitting in the center of the web,
listening intently, as was his wont, and he called softly to the star
maidens, saying: "Light as air is my web, but it is strong as steel."

The star maidens crept lightly towards the web and found a
long ladder, and they went down it, one after the other, until they
reached the earth beside the forest pool which they loved. The
moon shone softly through the trees, and blue lotus blooms, float-
ing on the pool, shed their sweet odors on the air. Casting off their
garments, the star maidens stole into the pool and bathed in it. The
waters were cool and sweet, and the spray broke from their fingers
like gleaming pearls.

It chanced that a hunter slept near the pool. He dreamt that
celestial beings disturbed the waters, and his heart yearned to see

them. So deeply did he yearn that he awoke suddenly. Raising himself on this elbow, he looked towards the gleaming water and saw the peerless star maidens. Then he crept round the blanks of the pool unit he reached the place where their gleaming garments lay amidst the bushes. One of the garments he lifted up. It had been woven with fine threads of silver and gold, and embroidered with gems of many colors. A large red ruby, which shone in the darkness, lay above the left breast, and it was shaped like a heart. Said the hunter: "the maiden who wears this gem must be true and steadfast and gentle. I would she were my bride."

When he had spoken thus, he crept back to the place where he had lain sleeping, keeping possession of the gleaming robe, and listened awhile to the music of the waters which the star maidens made as they bathed in the pool.

As dawn drew nigh, the King of Spiders called to the star maidens, saying: "Light as air is my web, but it is strong as steel. Alas! When the sun comes forth, his steeds will trample it underfoot."

The maidens heard the words of warning, and left the pool. Two of them seized their garments and put them on, and climbed up the invisible ladder of the web; but the third, who was the youngest and most beautiful, searched in vain for the robe of silver and gold which was embroidered with gems. Without it she was unable to return to her home, and she went about lamenting until the sun horses rode forth and trampled under foot the web of the King of Spiders.

Then birds awoke, and they sang to the star maiden, saying: "The hunter has taken away your robe, and lies pretending to slumber beneath the banyan tree."

Their words were heard by the disconsolate maiden, and she went towards the tree, clad in garlands of blue lotus blooms which she had gathered from the pool. She found the hunter, and, addressing him, said: "Give me back my robe of silver and gold which is embroidered and I will grant you any wish your heart may desire."

Said the hunter: "I will not give you back the robe which I have concealed, nor do I claim fulfillment of a wish from you. Be my bride and let us dwell here for ever."

The star maiden, having been robbed of her garment which gave her power over all the element was unable to leave the earth, and she become the hunter's bride. He loved her dearly; her voice was sweeter to hear than the voice of the kokila,[1] (The Indian cuckoo. Pronounce Ko-Kee'la) and her beauty was like that of the blue lotus. Together the hunter and his bride lived happily for seven years. Every day he went forth and found food for her, and at eventide they sat talking with one another. On moonlight nights the star maiden loved to sit beside the blue lotus pool, and often she cast eyes of love towards the stars. In her heart she longed to return to the Celestial regions, and she treasured also the hope that her two sisters would come again to bathe among the lotuses. But although the King of the spiders wove nightly the web which reached from the heavens to the earth, the star maidens did not return to bathe in the forest pool.

Three sons were born, and the star maiden loved them dearly. The first she called Star Gleam, the second she called Silver Bright, and the third Blue Lotus. Then a daughter was born, and the name she got was Ruby Heart.

One day the hunter spoke to his wife and children, saying: "I must travel towards the city of my birth, because it has come to my knowledge that my father is dying."

The star maiden said: "What if you should be slain by some wild beast? The way you must travel is long and dangerous. Do not leave us, O my husband."

"Gladly would I tarry beside you," the hunter answered, "but I cannot leave my father to die alone. He has no other son but me. I will close his eyes in peace, and after his funeral ceremony is performed, I will return again never to part with you until death call me."

Said Star Gleam: "Let me go with you, for fain would I see my grandsire."

"You must remain here," the hunter said, "and guard my house. Robbers may come and seek to plunder it."

Said Star Gleam: "Let me but accompany you a short distance, and I will return speedily and keep watch over the house until you return."

"So be it," answered the hunter.

Then he took his departure, promising to return in seven days. Star Gleam accompanied him until they reached the edge of the forest; then the hunter said: "Now return to our home and keep watch over it. Hear are the keys of all the chambers."

Star Gleam took the keys which is father gave him.

Said the hunter: "You may enter every chamber except one,

and that is the small upper chamber, which is opened with the golden key."

Star Gleam made answer: "I will do your bidding, O my father."

Said the hunter: "Now let us part, and each go his way. Be true and fearless of heart, and await my return."

Star Gleam went back through the forest, and when he reached his home he found his mother weeping at the doorway. He spoke to her and asked: "What ails you? Have no fear of robbers, for I will guard you against them."

The mother answered: "I have no fear of robbers."

"Then why do you weep?" asked Star Gleam.

"Because I shall never see your father again," she replied softly.

"He has gone to his own country, but will return soon," remarked Star Gleam. "No robber will do him harm, for he is strong and skilled in shooting arrows."

Said his mother: "I too must go to my own country, but will not return again to live here."

"Alas! do not speak thus," Star Gleam moaned. "Why would you leave us all, who are so happy here?"

Said his mother: I have no desire to leave you, Star Gleam, nor Silver Bright, nor Blue Lotus, and it would break my heart to leave Ruby Heart."

Her words made Star Gleam happy, for he thought his mother, whom he loved very dearly, had changed her mind and would never go away.

That night Star Gleam was awakened from sleep by hearing sweet bird-like voices calling in the moonlight: "Little sister, return; little sister, return with us. The King of spiders has spun his web, which is as light as air and as strong as steel."

Then his mother, who was singing Ruby Heart to sleep, answered, seeming still to sing to her little daughter:

O who would leave my Ruby Heart,
    My sweet, my pretty Ruby Heart?
    I ne'er will leave my Ruby Heart,
    To wander far away.

The voices outside sang in answer:
    O take with you your Ruby Heart,
    Your sweet, your pretty Ruby Heart,

> O you can take thy Ruby Heart
> To be your fairest gem.

Then his mother was silent, and the voices out side rose again:

> Return, return, O sister dear,
> The web is woven in the air;
> Oh! all the stars have wept for you,
> Since you did steal away.

Ruby Heart awoke from sleep and cried softly, and her mother sang again:

> Sleep, O sleep, my Ruby Heart,
> I cannot leave my Ruby Heart;
> My robe is lost, my Ruby Heart,
> And hid I know not where.

The little girl was soothed to sleep. For a time there was silence. Then once more the sweet voices outside rose in song, and Star Gleam heard them singing:

> If you would find the golden key
> To open the door forever closed-
> If you would find the golden key,
> You would not mourn again.

So soft and sweet were the voices that Star Gleam fell asleep, as he slept, he dreamt that two beautiful maidens came to him, saying: "Open the door of the upper chamber so that you mother may weep no more."

In the morning he spoke to his mother, and said: "Last night I heard voices raised in song, calling you to leave us."

The mother answered answer: "You must have dreamt this." Then she sat down to weep.

But Star Gleam was sure he had not been dreaming. All day long he thought of the songs he had heard sung, and when evening came on, he said to himself: "I will look into the upper chamber and discover what is there that makes my mother unhappy."

He was alone in the house at the time, for his mother had gone to bathe Silver Bright, Blue Lotus, and Ruby Heart in the forest pool. When he turned the key in the lock and opened the door, he perceived the robe of silver and gold which was embroidered with gems. It shone in the dark chamber as the stars shine in the heavens at night. Amazed with its beauty, he lifted it up and carried it down so that his mother might see it.

Before long his mother returned, and Star Gleam said: "I have found a beautiful robe. If you will put it on a little while, I am sure it will take away you sorrow."

His mother laughed sweetly, and her eyes lit up with joy when she saw the robe. Lifting it up, she drew it round her body. Then all her children laughed and danced with joy because she was so beautiful.

Said the star Gleam: "Every evening I will bring down the robe to you, O mother, until my father returns. Then I will prevail upon him to give it to you."

His mother answered: "Let me wear it tonight while I sing little Ruby Heart to sleep."

Said Star Gleam: "Very well, but I must lock it up again tomorrow."

That night, while Star Gleam lay awake in his bed, he heard the voices singing outside again in the soft moonlight:

Return, return, O sister dear,
    The web is woven in the air;
    Oh! all the stars have wept for you,
    Since you did steal away.

There was silence for a time. Then his mother's voice rose in song But it seemed to him that she sang from for away:

Sleep, O sleep, my Ruby Heart;
    I cannot leave my Ruby Heart;
    Oh! I will keep my Ruby Heart
    To be my fairest gem.

He desired to rise up and look out into the night, but heavy sleep fell upon him, and he did not awake until after the sun rose. Remembering the songs he had heard sung, he hastened to speak to his mother regarding them, but to his surprise was unable to find her anywhere in the house. "She has gone to the forest pool of the blue lotus," he thought. So went to the pool and wondered that he could not see her. When he returned to the house, he discovered that Ruby Heart had vanished also. His heart was filled with fear. "Alas!" he exclaimed, "robbers have come singing sweet songs, and have stolen away my mother and Ruby Heart. They have stolen also the robe of silver and gold which is embroidered with gems." Silver Bright and Blue Lotus mourned for their lost mother, and Star Gleam was unable to comfort them. All day they wept, searching the forest, and often they called: "Mother, O mother, return to your cnildren. How can you wander away and leave us? We are hungry and afraid. Oh! Return to us once again."

Star Gleam wept also, but not so much as Silver Bright and Blue Lotus: for his sorrow was mingled with fear of what his father would say and do when he returned to find that the command he had given had been broken. "Would I had never opened the upper chamber with the golden key!" moaned Star Gleam. "Because I have disobeyed my father, all this sorrow has fallen upon us."

That night when Star Gleam was putting his two brothers to bed, the door opened and his mother entered the house, wearing the robe of silver and gold which was embroidered with gems. Silver Bright and Blue Lotus ran towards her, uttering shouts of joy, and said: "All day we have moaned for you. We are hungry and afraid."

Said the mother:" Be not afraid. Although you did not see me, I was watching over you. I have brought you sweet food to eat."

Then she spread before them Celestial fruits which the children devoured with happy hearts.

Star Gleam did not eat. He spoke to his mother, saying: "where is Ruby Heart? Why did you go away from us? You promised not to leave us here alone."

Said his mother: "My sisters are singing Ruby Heart to sleep. I could not remain here because I had to go my own country, Tomorrow night I will come back again with food."

Star Gleam wept and said: "I dread to think of my father's return. He will be angry with me for opening the upper chamber and taking out the robe you are wearing. Leave it here, therefore, and when he returns I will prevail upon him to give it to you."

Said his mother: "Eat of the fruit first. We will talk of this matter afterwards."

When Star Gleam had eaten of the fruit, his heart become joyful and he forgot about the golden key and the upper chamber, and his father's command. It made him glad to gaze upon his mother clad in the beautiful robe. He believed that she would never leave him again, and he went to his bed with a happy mind. Before long he fell asleep, but he awoke again in the middle of the night. He heard voices calling:

Return, return, O sister dear,
> The web will break when day is come.
> Thy Ruby Heart is moaning loud
> Because you are not hear.

His mother was singing to Blue Lotus, who had wakened from sleep, and Star Gleam heard her sing:

Sleep, O sleep, Blue Lotus dear,
I cannot leave you here alone;
It breaks my heart to hear you cry
When I am far away.

Star Gleam said to himself: "Tomorrow I will prevail upon my mother to bring back Ruby Heart, so that we may all live together happily as before." But when he awoke in the morning he hound that this mother had vanished, talking Blue Lotus with her. Silver Bright wept and moaned for his mother and Blue Lotus and Ruby Heart; But Star Gleam said to him: "Do not sorrow. When night comes Mother will return to us." But Silver Bright could not be comforted, and long before the day was done his eyes were swollen with weeping.

Darkness came on at length, and the stars shone brightly overhead. Then the door opened, and Silver Bright saw his mother. He ran to her arms, crying: "All day long I have wept for you. Do not leave me again. Take me with you to the new home, for it is lonely here without you and Blue Lotus and Ruby Heart."

His mother kissed him and gave him to eat of Celestial fruit, and he was happy once again.

Said star Gleam, speaking to his mother: "You have taken away Ruby Heart and Blue Lotus, and now are going to take Silver Bright also. What will I say to my father when he returns home?"

"Eat this fruit first," his mother answered, "then we can talk together regarding this matter."

Star Gleam was faint with hunger, and he ate the fruit. When he did so, he forgot his sorrow and rejoiced to be with his mother, and to hear her voice, which was sweeter than the voice of the kokila.

He went to his bed and lay down to sleep. But he awoke before dawn, and heard the voices outside singing:

Return, return, O sister dear,
The web will break when day in come.
Blue Lotus and thy Ruby Heart
Are calling now for you.

His mother sang to Silver Bright, who had begun to cry, waking from his sleep:

Sleep, O sleep, my Silver Bright,
I cannot leave you, Silver Bright.
It Breaks my heart to hear you cry
When I am far away.

Heavy sleep again fell upon Star Gleam. He slept until long after dawn, and when he awoke and rose up, he found that he was alone in the house. So he sat down and wept, bemoaning his fate. All day long he wept, and before night came on, his mother entered the house.

Said Star Gleam: "Where are Ruby Heart, Blue Lotus, and Silver Bright? Why do you stay from me? Were we not all happy here together? When my father returns, his heart will be filled with sorrow he will punish me, because I have disobeyed his command and opened the upper chamber with the golden key." His mother spread out Celestial fruit before him and answered: "Eat first, then we will speak regarding this matter." Said Star Gleam: "I will not eat until my father returns again."

His mother tried to comfort him, and said: "Do not stay here any longer. I will take you with me to my own country, in which your brother and your sister are now well content to dwell."

Said Star Gleam: "Once I disobeyed my father's command, and it has brought me much sorrow. Never again will I do so. He bade me guard the house until his return. Ask me not, therefore, to go away."

His mother answered: " Tomorrow your father will come here. Say to him that I have returned to my own country, because I have found my robe of silver and gold which is embroidered with gems. Say also, that spirits came to you in a dream and bade you to open the upper chamber so that I might cease to sorrow. All these years since I left my home I have sorrowed in secret. I cannot again return to dwell here."

When she had spoken thus, the hunter's wife vanished from before her son's eyes, and ascended the invisible ladder of the King of the Spiders, which reached from the heavens to the earth. Star Gleam lay down to sleep, and next morning sat waiting until his father returned. All day long he waited, and when evening was coming on, he beheld him walking towards the house through the forest.

Said Star Gleam: "Alas! O my father, I am not worthy to live because I have disobeyed your command. Spirits come to me in my sleep and commanded me to open the door to the upper chamber so that my mother might cease to sorrow. I opened the door, and found the robe of silver and gold which was embroidered with gems. I took it out and gave it to my mother. And she was glad. But she went away that night when voices called for her, and will not return here again."

The hunter wept to hear what his son said. Then he answered: "I would that you had obeyed my commands. But as you have been punished by the loss of your mother, and with fear that I should smite you I forgive you. Let us dwell together happily with Ruby Heart, Blue Lotus and Silver Bright, and perhaps some day your mother may return home again."

"Alas!" cried Star Gleam, "my mother took Ruby Heart with her on the night she put on the robe of silver and gold which is embroidered with gems."

Said his father: "Sorrowful indeed am I, because Ruby Heart has been taken away. But it is better she should remain with her mother, for she is but a babe. Let us dwell together happily with Blue Lotus Bright."

"Alas!" cried Star Gleam; "my mother returned again and took away first blue lotus and then Silver Bright. Last night she came for me, but I said I would wait here for you."

His father wept and embraced his son, and said: "You have erred once and suffered much. But you have learned that obedience to a father is a high virtue which elevates a son, and because you have learned that, my heart is filled with thankfulness. Here let us dwell together. Do not leave me until death calls me away. Promise me that, my faithful Star Gleam."

Said Star Gleam: " I promise never to leave you, nor will I ever disobey your commands again, for disobedience to a father brings much sorrow."

So it came about that Star Gleam lived in the forest which his father. He went forth with him in the evening. But when night came on, and before he lay down to sleep, he often went outside to gaze up at the shining stars, and we wondered which was his mother and which was Ruby Heart, and which was Blue Lotus and which was Silver Bright. In his heart he longed to see the lost ones once again.

A year went past, and then a day came when his father called to Star Gleam in the middle of the night, saying: "Come to me, my son, for my life is almost spent."

The boy arose and went to his father, and tried to comfort him.

"Your lips are parched, O my father," he said. "I will bring you drink. Today we traveled too far, and you are weary. Tomorrow we will rest here, and before long you will grow strong again."

Said the father; "I fain would drink cold water." Star Gleam drew water from the forest pool of the blue lotus, and his father drank it. Then he lay down as if to sleep, and his son sat watching over him the whole night long. But before dawn broke in the east, the hunter died and Star Gleam wept aloud.

In the morning he gathered wood to make a funeral pile, and, like a faithful son, performed the last ceremony for his dead father. When all was finished he said: "I have now no desire to remain here any longer, but I know not whither I can go. My heart is full of sorrow." He sat down on he ground and wept, and when night came on he had not ceased weeping.

But when the stars came out, and the King of the Spiders had spun in the air the invisible web which reaches from the heavens to the earth, his mother returned to the house once again. Star Gleam lifted up his eyes and saw her with love in his heart.

"Sorrow not," his mother said, "but come with me to my own country."

Said Star Gleam: "Fain would I go, now that my father is dead."

His mother spread before him Celestial fruit, and when he had eaten of it, his heart was filled with joy.

The next morning two travelers came to the house, and entered it. They marveled greatly to find no one within, and they said one to another: "Let us dwell here until the owner returns."

No one ever returned again, and the travelers dwelt there until death called them.

It is told that on moonlit nights a merry group comes to bathe in the pool of the blue lotus, and that hunters have heard them calling one to another amidst the musical sound of the waters. And the names they usually repeat are "Star Gleam", "Blue Lotus", "Silver Bright", and "Ruby Heart". These are the children. And they call one of the bathers "mother", and two bright maidens call the mother "sister". And when dawn comes, a thin small voice failing through the air, entreats the merry-makers to return home are the horses of the sun will tread underfoot the invisible web which reaches from the heavens to the earth.

WONDERFUL ADVENTURES OF
TRANSFORMED ANIMALS

An ass, who was called Slow One, became very friendly with a hare, named Up-and-away, and they used to have conversation with one another.

"Have you ever noticed," remarked Up-and-away one evening, "how much we resemble one another in appearance? Our heads are of similar shape, and we both have long ears."

Said Slow One: "Now that you draw my attention to it, I must admit you are right."

"Of course," continued Up-and-away, "we have different habits, but that is due chiefly to our sizes. If you were as small as I am, you would no doubt be more like me. You require a long tail to drive off flies. I don't because I run so fast that they cannot catch me."

Said Slow One: "That is an advantage you have over me. I wish I were just your size so that I might escape these troublesome files. They torment me all day long."

"Another point of resemblance between us" remarked Up-and-away, "is that we eat similar food. We both love grass. As you have a larger mouth than I have, you eat thistles also. But if you were as small as me you couldn't."

Said Slow One: "I would gladly give up thistles if by doing so I could escape the flies."

"Suppose we change shapes for a time," suggested Up-and-away. "It would make us understand one another better. I have great desire to be big."

Said Slow One: "The idea is an excellent one. I should enjoy greatly running races with files. But how can we arrange the matter?"

"I know a magician," Up-and-away informed his friend, "who will enable us to change our forms. He lives in nearby forest on the banks of the sacred river."

Said Slow One: "Very well. Let us go and visit him at once. I am burning with anxiety to change my habits of life. There is nothing so enjoyable as a little novelty. An ass leads a very monotonous existence.

So the two friends set out at once to see the magician; and when they had made known to him their request, he said: "I am willing to transform you both as you desire. But remember this: I cannot change you back to your proper forms again unless you are both agreeable that such should be done. You will understand therefore that there are risks to be considered."

Said Slow One: "We have always been good friends. Never have we had a difference of opinion regarding anything. I am ready to take the risk."

"So am I," chimed in Up-and-away. "My friend need have no fear that I will not readily consent to reassume my form as soon as he asks me to."

"Friendship is a beautiful thing," remarked the magician. "It smooths over all difficulties. This would indeed be a pleasant world if all living creatures were as friendly as you both are."

Having spoken thus, he immediately transformed the animals, and the ass became a hare and the hare, an ass.

Said Slow One: "How pleasant the change is to me! I feel light-hearted and merry. See how I can run."

As he spoke, he leapt nimbly in the air and scampered out of the forest. He sat down in the middle of a field to think.

Up-and-away followed his friend, and when he reached him, said: "I am enjoying myself very much. It is pleasant to have such long legs. I can see a greater distance now than ever I did before. My enemies cannot approach me unawares any longer."

Said Slow One: "You will have to undertake my work, of course. In a short time my master will come to lead you to the market, and will place a load upon your back."

" I will enjoy that very much," answered Up-and-away. "I feel so strong and able. I could carry a mountain on my back."

"As for me," Slow One sighed, "I won't be able to carry anything. But I'll spend a pleasant time wandering about in perfect freedom and running races with flies."

I don't mind the files," said Up-and-away. "It is excellent sport lashing them with my long tail. What a useful thing a long tail is! The first idle day I have I will spend it killing files. I believe I can kill every fly in the world."

They had wandered back to their old haunts by this time, and Up-and-away looked down the road saw a man coming.

"I must go and hide myself," he remarked. "One of my enemies is approaching."

Said Slow One: "Nonsense! That man is not an enemy. He is your master. Allow him to lead you away. He wants to place a load on your back and drive you to the market."

"I had almost forgotten I was not still a hare," said Up-and-away. "How foolish of me! It is pleasant to think I need not have any fear of man."

"Said Slow One: "Well, good-bye for the present; I will meet you in the evening when your work is done. Then we can amuse one another by relating our experiences."

"Good-bye, my dear friend," Up-and-away exclaimed somewhat excitedly. "I hope you won't find things dull. I am looking forward with great pleasure to the new experiences I am going to have."

Said Slow One: "Before we part I had better give you a little advice. Don't be lazy. I was always inclined to be lazy. Walk quickly and obey your master's orders, and he will treat you well. If you are disobedient he will smite you with his long stave."

"Many thanks for your advice," remarked Up-and-away. "I will be a most exemplary ass. I will walk quickly, I can assure you, for I am longing to see what a market is like."

The owner of the ass drew nigh and seized hold of Up-and-away. He was greatly astonished to find that the animal was eager to obey him. Up-and-away trotted by his side towards the village, and the owner said: "What a splendid ass you are! I wonder what has come over you. If you go to the market as readily and smartly, I will give you an excellent meal."

He patted Up-and-away, who was greatly pleased with himself, placed a large burden on his back, and said: "Now, continue your good behavior and I'll keep my promise."

Up-and-away set off at a trot, and his master said: "Not so fast. I cannot keep up with you. Just walk at a smart pace and I will be well content."

Up-and-away did as he was commanded. He walked at a smart pace, and every few minutes his master praised him loudly. One after another he passed men with slow asses on the road, who had set out for the market before him, and to each of them he said: "What an excellent ass I have got! He has suddenly become a smart and willing animal."

Each man to whom he spoke said: "Your ass is an example to very other ass;" and each of them belabored his ass with a stave because it would not keep pace with Up-and-away.

All went well until the market-town was reached. Up-and-away was so much interested in what he saw, and so greatly flattered by his master's praises, that he though nothing of the load upon his back. But suddenly he saw a dog scampering towards him. Forgetting he was no longer a hare, he suddenly darted away and scampered off the road and across a field. His master shouted after him: "Come back, come back; where are you going? What trick is this you are playing on me?"

Up-and-away sat down in the middle of the field to think. Then he suddenly realized that he had blundered and need have no fear of dogs. So he rose up and turned back to meet his master, feeling very much ashamed of himself.

The man was angry and no sooner did he reach the runaway them he struck him with his stave several times, exclaiming: "Don't play tricks on me. Do you think I have nothing to do but run after you like this? See all the people are laughing. If you ever repeat this behavior, I'll break your back for you."

The blows he gave to Up-and-away were very painful, and the animal wept bitterly. Observing his sorrow, the man said: "I see you regret your folly. Very well, I forgive you. Now, come away and make up for lost time."

Up-and-away set out at a Quick pace, and before long reached the market-place. He was beginning to feel weary and perspired freely, and was glad when he was given a rest. When the load was taken from his back he sat down on his haunches like a hare and began to think.

Several boys gathered together, and pointing towards Up-and-away, exclaimed one to another: "Did you ever see such an amusing ass? How like a hare he is! Come and have some fun with him."

The boys began to throw stones at Up-and-away, who grew greatly alarmed; and springing to his lags, ran off through the streets. He scampered as fast as the wind, upsetting everything he came into contact with. An old woman sat at a corner selling all her oil. Next he collided with a fruit stall and scattered the fruit. Running down a side street, he overthrew two men, and then ran into a jeweler's shop and crouched in a corner to rest.

There was great excitement in the market down. The owner of the ass was amazed and angry, and ran after Up-and-away, followed by a large crowd. No sooner did he find his affrighted ass than he began to smite him with his stave.

Said the oil-seller: "You must pay for my oil."

Said the fruit-stall keeper: "You must pay for my fruit."

Said the two men who were overthrown: "You must pay damages for the injuries we have received."

Said the jeweler: "You must pay also for the loss I have sustained by the ass entering my shop and breaking so many things."

The owner of the ass heard them all with dismay, and answered: "I am not to blame. The boys tormented the ass and caused him to behave in this manner. I will go before the king and claim justice."

So they all went before the king, and when he heard what each of them said, he gave his judgment: " No ass would behave as this ass has done unless it had been greatly alarmed. It is evident that the boys are to blame for what has happened. Therefore the parents of the boys must pay for all the damages which have been done, and they must compensate the owner of the ass also."

The owner of the ass was so greatly delighted at the king's decision that he patted the ass and kissed him, saying: "My dear and faithful servant, I have treated you very badly. But as soon as we return home I will reward you as I promised."

Having sold his goods and received the money for compensation as the king commanded, the owner of the ass set homeward in his spirits, riding on the back of Up-and-away. "What a profitable journey this has been!" he exclaimed with glad heart, and began to sing.

Up-and-away had forgotten all his sorrows and ran nimble along the highway. Everyone who saw him looked on with wonder. "Was there ever such an ass in the world?" they exclaimed. "See how be runs. His master does not require to use his stave. This is no ordinary ass."

Up-and-away behaved well for a time, but beginning to feel weary, he thought he would like to shorten the way. So he suddenly turned from the road to scamper across a field.

"Hullo! Where are you going?" exclaimed his master But Up-and-away did not heed him. Thinking the man wanted him to go faster, he set out at a swift pace.

"This is really enjoyable," his master exclaimed. "The ass is full of fun, and deserves to get a little of his own way. He is taking a short cut home."

Leaving the field, Up-and-away entered a small wood which was situated a short distance from his master's house. Not being accustomed to have anyone on his back, he did not calculate properly the height of the clearances he should pass through. Soon after he entered the wood he darted under a low tree, and his master collided with a branch and fell heavily to the ground. Greatly alarmed at this accident, and fearing especially that he would be beaten again, Up-and-away scampered towards the place where he had parted from his friend.

"I have had enough of this life," he said. "It is too full of excitement for me. I must be changed back to my proper shape again."

As he spoke, he saw Slow One running towards him, followed by a dog. "Help me,!" cried the transformed ass. Up-and-away at once ran towards the dog and leapt upon it. The dog was greatly injured and scampered away. "How can I thank you, may friend!" exclaimed Slow One. "You have saved my life."

"I wish to resume my own from again," said Up-and-away excitedly.

"So do I," Slow One told his friend.

"As we are both agreed on this matter," Up-and-away said, "we had better hasten to the magician at once."

"So be it," agreed Slow One.

Now, while both animals are making their way to the man who accomplished their transformation, it would be well to relate what happened to Slow One while Up-and-away was experiencing his adventures in ass from.

Slow One was greatly pleased when he saw Up-and-way going away to perform a hard day's work. "What an idle time of it I shall have!" he exclaimed. "the weather is very pleasant and the flies won't worry me." He went for a scamper across a field, and enjoyed himself for a couple of hours. It was an amusing experience for him to pass through small holes in walls and fences, and to lie concealed behind tufts of long grass. But he soon grew tired of solitude, and thought he would go down to the village to see how other asses were engaged. He went boldly along the highway, but he had not gone far when he saw a dog advancing quickly. Wondering what the dog was chasing, he stood looking at it for a time. Then he realized that he himself was the object of the dog's desire. So he thought he had better run away. He turned to do so, and beheld another dog running towards him also. It was quite evident that he could not escape. How much he wished that he had retained his ass form so that he could kick out with his hind legs! Still he was brave, and stood coolly in the middle of the highway, hoping that the dogs would begin to fight and allow him to escape.

Greatly surprised to see a hare which did not scamper off at their approach, both dogs came to a standstill a few yards distant from Slow One. This amused the transformed animal very much, and he laughed" Hee-haw, Hee-haw", and looked from one dog to another. Never before did the dogs hear a hare laugh like an ass, and they shrank backwards, very much alarmed. Slow One Perceived that they were puzzled, so he raised his head and laughed "Hee-haw, Hee-haw" more loudly than before.

This was too much for the dogs. They turned right-about, greatly alarmed, and scampered off as fast as they were able to, Slow One sat where he was, laughing and holding his sides, until they vanished from sight. Then he crept from the highway and entered a field of young corn, where he browsed for a time.

Afterwards he resumed his walk towards the village. There came some children behind him, who ran towards him saying: "Let us catch the hare and kill him."

Slow One was alarmed at first, but he though he would try the same trick again. He sat down in the middle of the street and allowed the children to gather round. Then he began to laugh, "Hee-haw, hee-haw". The result was magical. There was not a child who would venture to lay hands on him. Seeing this, Slow One uttered a louder series of "Hee-haws", at which the children all turned and fled to their homes.

Slow One immediately went and hid himself, and it was well he did so, for a number of men and women came out of the houses with staves in their hands, looking for the laughing hare which had terrified the children.

"It is a Rakshasa," one cried.

"There is an evil spirit in the hare," another cried.

"We must slay him at once," they all agreed.

But they were unable to find Slow One who crouched behind a bush, listening to all that was being said. But he had to hide himself most of the day, so determined were the villagers to kill him. "When they forget about me," Slow One said, "I'll scamper sway. I know now why hares dislike villages."

He would have escaped unobserved just as evening was coming on, had not a cat smelt him out. Slow One scampered down an empty lane, but the cat followed him. So he thought he had better pushed for a moment and scare away his pursuer as he had scared the dogs and the children. Turning round suddenly he uttered a loud "Hee-haw, hee-haw". The cat faltered and looked puzzled. But cats are not easily deceived, and this one suddenly sprang towards the ass in hare form and would have caught him, had not Slow One swerved quickly and resumed his flight.

Then, fortunately for him, a dog sprang out against the cat. For a few seconds there was a lively fight, which ended in the cat running up a pole and remaining up the top if it.

Observing that the hare was still running, the dog turned his attention form the cat and followed the chase. Slow One paused and looked round, and seeing it was a dog who now pursued him, laughed "Hee-haw". But unfortunately for the transformed animal, this dog was deaf and did not falter in his quest. Slow One had to resume his flight, and was being hard pressed when he beheld his friend Up-and-away, who attacked and drove away the dog, as has been related.

When Slow One and Up-and-away reached the magician they requested him to change them back to their proper shapes again. This he did most readily, and the animals thanked him very much.

Said Up-and-away: "Now I must go off and feed, for I am very hungry."

Said Slow One: "How pleasant it is to be an ass again. I must go down to the village to meet my master. I long to see him, now that I need no longer fear the dogs and cats and children."

Said Up-and-away: "I have no desire ever to enter the village again. So good-bye for the present."

Slow One wandered along the highway towards the village, and beheld his master coming towards him, carrying a long stave in his hand. "Here you are, you rascal," the man exclaimed. "A pretty trick you played me. My back aches with the fall I got, so I will make your back ache also."

The man smote the ass heavily for a time, and when he grew weary, said: "Now that you have been punished for your folly, I will keep my word and award you for your good conduct. Come with me and I'll give you an excellent feed."

He led the ass towards his house and gave him a generous quantity of grain to eat. The poor animal, whose back ached very sorely, devoured his meal; and when he was done, said to himself: "Why I have been first beaten and then fed so well, I have not the least idea. But when one delegates his duties to another he must be prepared for anything. In future I had better attend to my own affairs and not risk my reputation by allowing another to look after them."

Then the ass's master came out and began to pat the animal, saying: "After all, you have dined well to-day. When next you go to the market I hope you will run as swiftly as you did today; but remember that if you play any tricks on me, I will beat you until you bones come through you skin."

The ass turned away with a sad heart. "I must run to the market, must I?" he exclaimed with sorrow. "Alas! what folly to allow a hare to change the ancient and honorable customs of my kind. It will take me some time to convince my master that asses must remain asses until the end of the world, and that if he wants a four-footed animal to run, he should employ a horse."

Next morning his master came towards him, accompanied by a stranger, who said, "So this is the ass you had at the market yesterday.

"It is," his master made answer.

"I will purchase it from you," said the stranger.

"How much will you give for it?" the other asked.

"The price of five asses," said the stranger.

"Say twice five and he is yours," the master suggested.

"Very well," agreed the stranger, "I will give you the price of ten asses." And he did so.

The master bade his ass farewell, and the stranger led him away. But when he discovered that Slow One was no better than any other ass, he smote him so severely that he broke the stave over his back.

Said the ass: "This is the beginning of the trouble. I wonder where it will end. A little spark often sets a whole jungle on fire."

So he went to the magician and laid the whole matter before him. "What am I to do?" Slow One asked.

"If you can find any animal to change shapes with you for a little time," the magician said, "you may get relief from your troubles."

This advice was not pleasing to the ass, but he went into the jungle and looked about him until he found a tiger. To this fierce animal he related all his troubles, and the tiger Asked: "Is your new master nice and fat?"

"He is, indeed, both nice and fat," answered the ass.

"Then," said the tiger," I will change shapes with you for a single day."

Together they went to the magician, and when they had changed their shapes, the tiger in ass form went to the village. There Slow One's new master seized him and dragged him into the forest, where he cut a long stave. He began to smite the transformed animal. But the tiger-ass seized the man and ate him up. Several people observed this happening, and ran towards the village to tell what had occurred. The tiger then went to look for the ass, and when he found him, said: "Came, let us change shapes again." The ass was only too willing to do so, because he had been trying to eat grass and thistles, and found that a tiger's teeth were very unsuitable for such a purpose.

Slow One, as soon as he had resumed his ass form, returned to the village. He found, however, that everyone ran away from him, greatly alarmed. So he wandered towards the forest and took up his abode there, and as nobody was inclined to claim him, he lived happily for the rest of his days, wandering about as he chose and holding converse with all sorts of animals, wild and tame.

Meeting the hare one, day he asked: "How are you getting on, my friend?"

Said Up-and-away: "Very well indeed I am glad to be a hare. Never again will I change shapes with you."

Said the ass: "I am glad to hear you say so. I, too, am content to remain as I am. The happiest person is he who is true to himself, and does not pretend to be someone else. Hares are best as hares, and asses as asses."

HOW TWO MEN TRICKED THE RAKSHASAS

There were once two beggars. The one was blind and the other was deaf. The names they had were See Naught and Hear Little. One day See Naught bawled into the ear of his friend, saying: "We will never make our fortunes if we spend our time asking for alms. Let us set forth in search of adventures. As neither of us is able to do this by himself, we should form a partnership. What I have you lack, and I lack what you have. It is evident that if we combined our faculties we could remedy our defects."

Hear Little was quite agreeable to enter into a partnership. So the couple left the town in which they had begged for years, and wandered towards the jungle.

"When you hear anything special, let me know," the deaf one said.

"When you see anything particular, tell me," said the blind one.

They had not gone far when See Naught heard a donkey braying. "There's one strayed donkey over there," See said; "we will require one to carry anything we find."

Hear Little walked in the direction indicated until he saw the strayed donkey. He seized the bridle and led it away. They walked on a while, and Hear Little remarked: "I see an ants' nest."

"Catch a few ants," See Naught said, "they may be useful to us."

Hear Little caught three ants and placed then in a snuff-box, and together the men resumed their journey. They walked on until it grew dusk, and Hear Little said: "It is almost night and we have not reached a house yet. This is unfortunate, especially as a storm is brooding."

"I will lead the ass in darkness," See Naught told him. "Day and night are both the same to me. Follow where I lead until you see something."

It grew very dark, and Hear Little seized the donkey's tail and followed his friend's lead. At length the storm broke out in fury. Rain fell in torrents, lightning flashed with great brilliance, and the thunder bellowed loud.

"How dreadful is the lightning!" said the man who could see.

"I have no fear of the lightning," the blind man remarked; "what worries me is the terrible thunder."

"The thunder does not trouble me at all," said Hear Little. "The rain is the next worst thing to the lightning. I wish we could find a house.

There is a house near here," See Naught exclaimed. "I know that, because I can feel the imprints of many footsteps left by people who have come and gone this way. Those which follow the direction in which we travel are deep, and those turned towards us are light. Heavy feet go homeward wearily; light are the feet of those who leave home."

"I sometimes think," his friend commented, "that blind men see more than men with perfect eyesight. To hear you speak one might imagine you had eyes in your feet."

"Can't you see the house?" the other asked impatiently.

As he spoke a vivid flash of lightning illuminated the jungle, and Hear Little saw in front of them a lofty building.

"Ha! You are right," he cried, "here's a house which is big enough to shelter a giant."

"Did I not tell you we were not far from a place of shelter?" shouted See Naught.

Said Hear Little: "Don't boast too much about it. Perhaps before the night is past you will need my help as much as I need yours."

They entered the house with the donkey, and finding that it was empty, shut the door and bolted it securely.

Now this tall building was the home of a family of Rakshasas (demons). They had gone to prowl in the jungle in search of wandering human beings so that they might devour them. Not long after the two men and the donkey entered their house they returned, because they feared that Indra, the king of gods, would slay them with his thunderbolt. It surprised these night-prowlers greatly to find the door shut.

Said the biggest Rakshasa: "Hoo! ho! hee! hee! Manush gandha! I smell fresh human flesh. There are men inside. I'll eat them up and drink their blood."

Then he knocked at the door with his fists and kicked it with his feet, roaring as loud as a lion: "Open the door. What right have you to enter my house? Open the door, I say; open the door." See Naught trembled when he heard the Rakshasa's terrible voice. Hear Little peered through the keyhole, and when a flash of lightning went past and he saw the Rakshasas, he was struck with fear.

"Open the door, open the door," roared the fierce monster until his voice grew hoarse.

See Naught grew brave when the Rakshasa ceased calling for very weariness; so he shouted:
"Who is making that noise outside my door? It is very late and I can't allow you to enter. Go away or you will awaken my little boy."

"Open the door," repeated the monster. "The house you are in is mine. I am Rakshasa, and if you disobey me I'll break down the door and eat you up."
Said the blind man: "I am very angry with you. If I open the door I will eat you instead. You open the door I will eat yourself instead. You may be a Rakshasa, but I am the Bakshasa."

"The Bakshasa?" Exclaimed the Rakshasa. "What is that? I never heard of a Bakshasa."
Said the blind man: "How ignorant you are! Bakshasa is the grandfather of all the Rakshasas. This house is mine. I built it before you were born."
The Rakshasas outside began to discuss the matter, and they said one to another: "If the grandfather of all of us in inside, we dare not enter without his permission."

Then one of them who was not quite convinced remarked: "What if we are being deceived? The voice which speaks to us is not very strong."
The biggest Rakshasa went back to the door and knocked loudly again.
"Have you not gone away yet?" cried the blind man. "Do you wish me to come out and punish you?"
Said the biggest Rakshasa: "if you are our grandfather, please let us hear you roar."

"Very well," the blind man answered. "Just listen."

He put his hand in the pocket of the deaf man and pulled out the snuff-box. Opening it, he dropped the ants into the donkey's right ear. Being very hungry, angry and frightened all at once, the ants began to bite ferociously, and the donkey roared with pain, making a hideous din.

I thought the ants would be useful to us," the blind man remarked.

"What a dreadful voice the Bakshasa has!" the Rakshasas said one to another; "If he roars like that to amuse himself, he must be terrible indeed to hear when he is angry."

Said the biggest Rakshasa: "Perhaps we had better go away."

"Wait a minute," another advised. "Although his voice is quite extraordinary, he may not be impressive to look upon. Frogs croak loudly and yet can do no harm."

"Very well," the biggest Rakshasa remarked. "I will speak to him again."

So he rapped at the door and called: "O Bakshasa, you have a splendid voice and we are all impressed very much by it. Before we go away we should like, however, to gaze upon your face."

"Stand back then," the blind man made answer.

The Rakshasas looked at one another with alarm, and retreated several paces. Meanwhile the deaf man stood on the donkey's back, while the blind man crouched between its fore legs. The ants renewed their fierce attack within the poor animal's right ear. Leaning forward, Hear Little opened the door slightly. Thinking he could escape his tormentors, the donkey thrust out his head and being unable to move forward, stood up on its hind lags and roared with agony. Hear Little waved his hands above the donkey's head, and See Naught clapped his hands below it.

All the Rakshasas were terrified to see the fierce Bakshasa with four arms and gaping Jaws, and to hear his angry roaring. For a moment they looked, then they darted away to hide themselves in the jungle. Louder and louder rose the repeated howls of the donkey, and the fleeing monsters thought their grandsire was following them.

Hear Little then leapt down and took the ants out of the donkey's right ear. That relieved the poor animal's sufferings and he grew silent.

Said See Naught: "Now that the demons have gone and the donkey has ceased to roar, I can get some sleep."

He lay down, and Hear Little lay down, and the donkey lay down also. Before long they were fast asleep and pleasant were their dreams.

Next morning Hear Little awoke early and began to prowl through the house. To his joy he discovered a great hoard of jewels and silver and gold. He returned to his friend and shook his from sleep. See Naught at once sprang up saying: "Have I slept too long? The sun has risen. I can smell the morning air. We had better resume our journey."

Hear Little told him of the treasure he had discovered and said: "There is a sufficient quantity to make us both very rich. Let us carry it all away.

They filled two large sacks of silver and gold, and placed them on the donkey's back. Then they tied up two small bundles of jewels, and See Naught carried the one while Hear Little carried the other. Leaving the house, they hastened to return by the way they had come.

Now the Rakshasas were watching the house from far off, and they saw the two men and the donkey leaving it, they realized that they had been tricked. So their leader cried out:

"Let us hasten after the men and devour them."

"And devour the donkey also," another said.

"And recover our treasure," exclaimed a third.

Hear Little looked round and saw six Rakshasas drawing high. "The monsters are pursuing us," he shouted to his friend. "We had better conceal the treasure among the bushes and climb up a tree."

This they did. They threw down their bundles and made the donkey crouch in long grass, as it was glad to do, for the yells of the Rakshasas terrified it very much. Then they climbed up a high tree. See Naught went first, and Hear Little pushed him from behind until he had crawled out on a branch.

Hear Little looked round and watched the Rakshasas approaching. One had a mouth like a tiger and eyes like saucers; another had long ears which stood high above his head; the rest were of varied shapes, and all were dreadful to look upon. The blind man was very brave because he could not see the monsters.

"We are quite safe here," he shouted to his friend. Said Hear Little: "We would be still safer if you moved forward a little further."

See Naught moved forward and the Rakshasas caught sight of him.

"We'll eat that one first," cried the one with the tiger's mouth, pointing at the blind man.

"Who are they going to eat?" See Naught asked his friend.

Said Hear Little: "They intend to eat the donkey first."

The Rakshasas gathered together under the branch on which the blind man lay, and the one stood on the other's shoulder to reach him. The long-eared monster was the highest and he stretched out his hands to seize See Naught, but was unable to reach him.

"Move forward a little further," Hear Little called to his friend. The blind man moved forward and caused the branch to bend down. Thinking he was about to fall, See Naught stretched out his hands and clutched wildly. By good fortune, his hand closed on the upright ears of the topmost Rakshasa. He held them with a firm grip.

See Naught bent down and seized one of the ears between his teeth.

"The monstar has begun to devour me," the Rakshasa shouted louder than before.

When the Rakshasa who stood on the ground heard that, he darted away, and all the others tumbled down in a heap. Having no idea what was happening, and fearing for their own safety, all the fallen monsters sprang to their feet and followed their companion who had taken to flight. Glancing round, they saw the long-eared Rakshasa dangling in the air and heard him shouting and screaming with terror and pain.

Hear Little laughed to see the monsters in flight, and spoke to his companion, saying: "Now let the last Rakshasa fall to the ground."

See Naught did so, and the monster limped away howling like a jackal, and causing his companions to run faster than ever.

"Come down now," Hear Little said to his friend, "we are quite safe."

See Naught did so, and then asked the deaf man what had taken place.

"It's a long story," said the fellow; "I will describe everything at a more convenient time. Meantime be satisfied with the knowledge that I have completely outwitted the Rakshasas and caused them to take speedy flight."

The two men then recovered the bags of jewels and the donkey, and went on their way.

When evening was coming on, they drew nigh to the town in which they had begged for years.

Said Hear Little: "Let us now divide the treasure between us."

"Very well," See Naught agreed. "We will take a half each."

Hear Little laid aside the greater part of the treasure for himself, and handing a small bundle to See Naught, said: "That is your share."

The blind man lifted up the bundle and exclaimed: "You are cheating me. There were two sackfuls on the donkey's back and each of us carried a bundle. Now you give me less than I myself took from the Rakshasa's home."

"No, no," protested Hear Little.

"I tell you," See Naught repeated, "that you are cheating me."

"Speak louder," said Hear Little. "I am dull of hearing."

See Naught made no answer, but struck his friend a violent blow on the right ear and another violent blow on the left ear. The result was magical. These two well-directed blows immediately restored the hearing of the deaf man. But he did not realize this all at once. He struck his friend two blows in return, one on the right eye and another on the left. Again the result was magical. The blind man had his eyesight restored at once. He leapt with joy, and said to his friend: "Now I can prove that you were trying to cheat me. I can see the full amount of treasure we carried away. You wish to secure the greater proportion to yourself."

Said the other: "It is joyful to be able to hear again. Let us be good friends and divide the Rakshasa's hoard into equal shares."

This they did, but when they opened the sack they found that all the gold and silver had turned to blocks of wood, and the jewels to small pebbles.

"Alas!" cried the man who had been deaf, "the Rakshasas have worked magic against us and robbed us of the treasure."

"Had we not quarreled one with another," the man who had been blind exclaimed, "we might have been rich man."

"Never mind," said the other," it was because we quarreled that I got back my hearing."

"Yes, yes," assented the man who had been blind," and I got back my eyesight. We should be thankful for our good fortune. Better are eyes that see than a sackful of gold."

"Better are ears that hear than a bag of jewels," his companion cried, and began to dance with joy.

Feeling very happy, the two friends returned to the town in which they had been accustomed to beg, arm in arm. Next day they related all that had occurred to the citizens, and they received many gifts. When the king heard of their doings, he sent for them and bade them repeat their stories to him. He was so greatly pleased with the men that he appointed them as sentinels at the palace, and there they lived happily for the rest of their days, for they had little to do and received plenty of food. No sentinel had keener eyes than the man who had been blind, and no sentinel could hear so well as he who had been deaf.

WISDOM IS BETTER THAN STRENGTH

A black snake took up its dwelling in the hollow of a tree, on a branch of which there was a crows' nest. The parent birds found that their new neighbor was a most undesirable one, for he crept up and stole their eggs, and if the eggs were hatched, devoured their young.

Said the mother crow: " I think we should leave this tree. We will never rear young ones so long as that snake dwells beside us."

"He pretends to be friendly," the father crow commented.

Said the mother crow: "Judging by his actions he is a false friend. Don't you remember the old saying?

"From friends who cause trouble,
From a snake-haunted house,
From slaves who are double,
From a quarrelsome spouse—
Speed the parting, O master,
Or you'll meet with disaster."

The father crow answered, saying: "Do not worry about the snake. He has exhausted my patience. I have quite made up my mind to get rid of him."

Said the mother crow: "Alas! Although your courage is admirable, your strength is limited. How can you expect to be successful if you wage a conflict with such a powerful enemy as the big black snake?"

"Trust in me," answered the father crow. "It is better to be wise than strong. The mind is the master of the body, and when the thoughts of mind are directed against the strength of the body, the mind always wins. Have you never heard how the clever hare overcame the great lion and caused his death?"

"No," the mother crow admitted. "What did the hare do?"

"Listen and I will tell you," said the father crow. And this was the story he related:

"There was once a fierce lion who lived in a mountain cave. He was as greedy as he was savage, and not only devoured many inoffensive animals, but even slew large number just because he loved to massacre. As time went on, his bad habits grew worse, and he cultivated no good ones. All the wild animals regarded him as a nuisance, and at length they held an assembly to consider what should be done. After a long discussion it was arranged to present the following petitions to the lion:

"We beg respectfully to make appeal to your Majesty to change you habits. Why do you cause so much unnecessary slaughter? Let us make offering to you every day of an animal, so that we who dwell near you and serve you may be able to perform our duties with decency and order."

The lion listened attentively to the petition, and answered: "Very well; if such is your desire I am quite willing to enter into this new arrangement. It will save me a good deal of trouble."

So the matter was arranged accordingly. Every day an animal was chosen by casting lot, and delivered up to the lion. The King of beasts was well pleased.

As it chanced, there came a day when the old hare, whose name was Long Ears, was chosen to be the victim. He accepted his fate without complaint, and said: "I can only die once. So I need not worry myself. And as the lion cannot do worse than kill me, I need not display any undue haste in approaching him."

The hare them set off towards the royal cave, walking slowly, apparently quite unconcerned.

On that day it happened that the lion was very hungry. Being hungry he was angry, and being angry he could not help being impatient. He waited for his victim, walking restlessly up and down the cave, and occasionally uttering low growls. When he saw the hare approaching he grew angrier than ever, not only because his meal was to be so·small, but also on account of the hare's leisurely movements. "What do you mean?" he roared. "How dare you keep me waiting when I am hungry? Explain."

Said the hare: "I must offer your Majesty my most sincere apologies. I regret very much that I have caused you any inconvenience, but, really, I am not to blame. On my way hither I met another lion. He desired to devour me, but I informed him I was intended for your Majesty. He scoffed at this and commanded me to swear an oath that I would come and inform you he desired to devour me instead, and when I did so, to return to him."

"The lion opened his eyes wide, growled fiercely, and said: "Lead me to this impudent imposter at once. I will show him who is monarch of this mountain."

"The hare bowed respectfully, and turning round about, ran towards a deep pool which was surrounded by a steep wall of rock. Standing on the edge of the rock, Long Ears said: "Here is your rival, O King of the mountain. Come and look at him."

The lion hastened to the hare's side, and, gazing down, saw his own image on the surface of the clear water. Snorting with fury, he at once leapt into the pool, thinking he was attacking his rival. Being unable to swim, he met with a speedy death.

"Then the hare returned to his friends and informed them of what had taken place. They all praised him for his wisdom, and the hare said: 'A sharp mind is the hare's salvation.'

"Such is the story of the lion and the hare," concluded the father crow.

"It is an entertaining story, indeed," remarked the mother crow. "But I do not see how you can lead the snake to a well and make him drown himself."

Said the father crow: "A snake cannot be overcome in the same manner as a lion. It is necessary to deal with each enemy in a special and suitable way. The lion was a king and was jealous of a supposed rival. Knowing the lion's weakness, the hare acted as he did and achieved success. A snake is not a king, and has great cunning. The ways to get rid of him is to attract his enemies. When they see him they will work according to my will."

"What do you propose to do?" asked the mother crow.

"Perhaps you have observed," the father crow said, "that the king's son is in the habit of bathing in our stream every morning. I have watched him carefully and have studied his habits. Before entering the water, he takes off a gold anklet and lays it on a flat stone. When he comes tomorrow morning, fly down and carry off this anklet and let it fall into the hollow of the tree in which the black snake lies asleep."

"Very well, I will do so," his spouse promised.

Next morning the king's son came to bathe in the stream. As soon as he had entered the water the mother crow flew down and carried off the gold anklet. The servants of the prince observed the happening, and they observed also that the crow dropped the anklet into the hollow of the tree. Without delay they hastened to recover it, and when they saw the black snake they at once killed him. Recovering the stolen ornament, they carried it to the prince. When the father crow returned in the evening, his spouse informed him of what had taken place, and he at once surveyed with thankful heart the body of their enemy.

"Was I not right?" he exclaimed. "Artifice is more efficacious than brute strength. A wise thought is the crow's salvation. He who observes gets knowledge, and he who has knowledge is able to act aright."

THE MYSTERY OF THE PALACE

On a day of a jackal's wedding—that is, a day when rain falls in sunshine—a king was hunting in a jungle, and slew a tiger and numerous lesser animals. Then he grew weary and entered a small but thick forest to find rest and shelter. A carpet was laid beneath a banyan tree, and he sat upon it, looking about him and pondering over many things. His servants had gone away to gather the game together, and for a time he was quite alone.

Suddenly he become aware that a beautiful maiden was moving about among the bushes not far from where he reposed. She was attired in many-colored garments and adorned with gems which flashed and sparkled like stars at midnight. Now she stood half-revealed like a Nag maiden (serpent maiden), waist-deep among newly blown flowers; anon she flitted out and in among the trees like the restless moon among scattered clouds on nights of storm; and sometimes she rushed momentarily in radiant splendor on an open space beneath an arch of greenery, looking wistfully about her, as if she sought to catch a glimpse of someone for whom she was anxiously making search.

Wondering who this peerless lady might be, the king rose and went towards her, but for a time she eluded him without seeming to be aware of his present. He called, but she did not answer; he ran to the right, and she appeared in the opposite direction; he ran to the left, and glancing round, saw her flitting about the place from which he had started. At length, however, be found her, sitting on the trunk of a fallen tree, surrounded by tangled veils of blossoming creepers, uttering doleful sounds as if she sorrowed in despair. He spoke to her softy, saying: "Who are you, O beautiful one, and where have you come from?"

With tears falling from her radiant dark eyes, she answered: "I am a princess from a far country, and I have been carried away by a Rakshasa. My father and mother are slain and the kingdom is laid waste. Here I wander alone, having escaped my enemies, but I know not where I should go to find shelter and protection from those I dread. When darkness comes on, the Rakshasas will hasten here and search for me."

Said the king: "Have no fear. I will protect you from all harm. I have never seen with my eyes a maiden so beautiful as you are. Come with me and live in my palace and be my chief queen."

The maiden looked with grateful face upon the king, and smiled sweetly. Whiter than river foam were her teeth, and they gleamed like mountain snow in sunshine. She said: "Well content am I to obey your wish, O mighty monarch. Lead me out of this forest before darkness comes on."

So it happened that the king took as his bride the beautiful maiden whom he met by chance, and he married her and she become the chief queen.

But this strange princess was no other than a female Rakshasa (demon), who had assumed such pleasing form with purpose to cause trouble and disharmony in a prosperous and well-governed kingdom, where justice was administered with mercy and care. It was hateful for the night prowlers of the forest to know that human beings lived happily, and were ruled over by a pious and high-souled king, who never neglected a religious rite and made generous gifts to holy men.

Not long after the deluging imposter was installed in the palace, she began to avenge herself on the innocent and worthy. Each night, when sleep lay heavily on old and young, and none were awake save a few watchman, she arose, and assuming some fearsome shape, went wandering through the streets. The food she received never satisfied her, on the first night that she stole forth she devoured two sheep. When she did so, the left some of the bones and wool at the door of the king's gardener's house, and split blood beside them. Next morning the owner of the sheep made complaint to the king, and the gardener was cast into prison.

Now the Rakshasa queen's reason for thus accomplishing the downfall of the gardener was because he was a man endowed with much wisdom. She had perceived that he suspected her. Often he watched her walking in the garden, with curious eyes. But the gardener had a friend in the Vizier, who went to the prison and said: "Why have you brought this disgrace upon yourself? Were you not prosperous and happy? The king trusted you and honored you, and yet you have become a law-breaker."

Said the gardener: "I am innocent of this charge. An enemy has implicated me by placing bones and wool on my doorway and spilling blood beside them."

"If you have an enemy," the Vizier said, "make known his name to me so that he may be watched."

Said the gardener: "Alas! I dare not utter my enemy's name, for I cannot prove anything against her. Yet my heart is convinced of her guilt."

"So your enemy is a woman," the Vizier commented. "Who is she? Inform me of your secret and I will not reveal it."

Said the gardener: "She is no other than the chief queen-the strange and beautiful woman whom the king found in the forest. Beware of her. Who knows what evil she may yet accomplish?"

The Vizier pondered over the man's words in silence, and said: "Speak to no one else regarding this matter. I will keep watch now that you have been removed."

Now it soon came about that the chief queen perceived that the Vizier eyed her with suspicion. So she resolved to bring him into disgrace. The king possessed several animals in which he took pride. These were four swift-footed steeds, each of which had the ten good marks, a white camel of peerless beauty and strength, and a mighty elephant of surpassing height and bulk. They were cared for by faithful servants who were responsible to the Vizier, while the Vizier was responsible for all the animals to the king.

One dark night the chief queen arose, and entering the royal stables, devoured two of the swift-footed steeds. She laid their hooves and portions of their hides outside the gate of the Vizier's house, and split blood beside them.

Great was the sorrow of the queen, and he sent for the Vizier and said: "You have neglected your duty. Two of my swift-footed steeds have been slain by someone in your house."

Said the Vizier, who was greatly alarmed for his own safety: "I will cast my servants into prison and set stronger guards over the stables."

"So be it," said the king.

Next night the chief Rani in her Rakshasa form went towards the stables. She worked magic against the watchmen, who were all thrown into a deep sleep, and devoured the other two horses. Then she said their hoofs, and portions of their hides, on the threshold of the Vizier's house, and spilt blood beside them.

Next morning the king was more sorrowful than ever, and he spoke to the Vizier: "Can I trust no one? Now all my fleet-footed steeds have perished, although you increased the guard and imprisoned your servants. If another disaster happens, I will have you put to death."

The Vizier went away with his heart full of grief. As he left the palace he caught sight of the chief queen and saw her smile. He was confident that the woman was his persecutor, yet he could not say it and was compelled to keep silence.

He spent the day making elaborate preparations to guard the remaining two favorite animals of the king, and resolved that he himself would keep watch also.

But when night came, the chief queen transformed herself into a bat and flew towards the stables. She slew four guards who stood fully armed beside the white camel; then devoured the beautiful animal, and passing over the guardhouse in which the Vizier sat, dropped the hoofs and portions of the skin before the door, and spilt blood beside them. Soon after midnight the Vizier left the guardhouse and went from watchman to watchman, speaking to each, and saying: "Has anyone come near?"

One after another the watchmen made answer: "No one has come near. Indeed, the only living creature we have heard was a little bat which few towards the stables and then flew back again."

The Vizier then entered the stables, and discovered to his horror that the watchmen who guarded the white camel had been slain, and that the camel could not be found anywhere. He raised the alarm and lights were brought. The watchman searched for the missing camel, and when they reached the door of the guard-house in which the Vizier had sat, they found its hoofs, portions of its skin, and saw the marks of blood beside them.

In the morning the Vizier hastened before the king and related all that had taken place. Said the grief-stricken king: "I cannot now trust even you. It is strange, indeed, that traces of the slain animals should be found on each occasion near to the places where you chanced to be. What is the meaning of this?"

The Vizier bowed his head and answered: "if your Majesty suspects that I have been unfaithful, command that I be put to death. So great is my sorrow that death seems to me now to be more desirable than life."

Said the king: "My heart is afflicted with doubt. I desire to believe in your innocence, yet all the proofs are against you. Have you no suspicion of who is working this evil in the darkness of night?"

The Vizier answered, saying: "No mortal could so deceive the watchman as to pass unobserved to and from the royal stabled. Last night the devourer of the camel flew though the darkness in the from of a bat."

Said the king: "Then why was the bat not slain? Command the guards who are set over the stables tonight to kill and every animal which may come near."

The Vizier promised that the guards would be increased, and they would receive the royal command to slay whatever moving thing approached the stables. Then he took his departure.

No sooner had he gone than the chief Rani approached the king and said: "Why is the Vizier not put to death? It is certain that he has accomplished all this evil."

"If the great elephant is slain," the king told her, "he will be executed forthwith."

In her heart the chief Rani rejoiced to hear the words, for she dreaded the Vizier.

That evening the Vizier released the gardener from prison and placed him among the guards who surrounded the stables. Then he went himself and sat near the great elephant, and gave that peerless animal dainties to eat from time to time, so that he might not lie down in slumber.

The gardener meanwhile sent for two friends to help him, having obtained the Vizier's consent to do so. One was named Hear All, because no sound escaped him, were it so faint as that made by an insect brushing its wings; the other was named See All, because he could perceive objects at night as well as another could in daylight. None of the other watchman had knowledge of these men's accomplishments.

Soon after midnight the chief queen transformed herself into a bat and flew towards the stables.

Said Hear All: "A bat comes near."

See All said: "It is not a bat, but a Rakshasa in bat form."

The gardener bade the archers to bend their bows and shoot the night bird, but no sooner had he spoken than it vanished. Aware of the danger that was in store for her, the chief queen transformed herself into a snake and crept through the grass.

Said Hear All: "A snake comes near."

See All said: "It is not a snake, but a Rakshas in snake form."

The gardener warned the guards, and they waited for the approach of the creeping reptile, but again the chief queen transformed herself; she become a mole, which burrowed under the ground. For a time there was silence, and the gardener asked Hear All if he heard anything, and the man answered: "No, not a living creature moves on the face of the earth nigh to us." Then he asked See All if he saw anything, and the man shook his head, saying: "Right there a little earth was tossed in the air by the wind some moments ago, but now I see nothing else in motion."

An hour went by. Then Hear All whispered: "I hear a burrowing sound beneath our feet. I fear that it is made by a Rakshasa in mole form."

Said the gardener: "Lead me to the place where you heard the sound, and I will dig for the mole."

Hear All did so, but when the ground was opened up, they found the tunnel made by the mole, but were unable to see the animal.

"It has retreated," the gardener said, extinguishing the light he held.

He rose up. Then Hear All whispered: "I hear an insect buzzing in the air."

Said See All: "It has flown towards the stables and entered at the keyhole of the door."

The insect was the queen, who had so cunningly eluded the watchmen. She crept into the stables and concealed herself in the crack of a brick near the roof, and there remained.

Said the gardener: "Bid the watchmen to catch a hundred spiders and bring them here."

The watchmen turned away to do so, but they had not gone far when they were called back. It came to the knowledge of the gardener that the queen had again changed her shape.

Said Hear All: "A little mouse is creeping through a hole in the wall."

See all looked the said: "I see the shadow of a mouse's tail."

Said Hear All: "Now it pauses, waiting."

See All said: "I see the tip of its whisker in yonder corner."

The gardener crept forward and placed himself between the mouse and the elephant and made ready to strike. Near him stood the Vizier. There ensued a long silence, and the watchmen grew weary. Then suddenly the queen changed her shape and sprang from the straw as a ferocious tiger. There was no further need for Hear All or See All. They turned and fled. The gardener fled also, and called the watchmen who were outside to bring arms so as to combat against the tiger. But the Vizier never moved. He drew his sword and waited for the tiger to strike, but the elephant, which tried to break loose, struck him soon with his trunk, and the faithful man fell heavily and became unconscious.

Larger and lager grew the tiger until she exceeded the elephant in bulk, filled the stable and pressed against the door. Then the monster devoured the elephant, leaving only the tusks and the tail and a pool of blood. The watchmen outside hewed the door with axes and thrust their spears through it, and one spear entered the right foot of the monster tiger, causing blood to flow freely.

Terrified lest she would be slain, the chief queen transformed herself into a bat and flew through a hole in the roof, and made her way towards the palace.

See All perceived that she entered through one of the palace windows.

When the watchmen entered the stables, they found that the elephant had been devoured and saw the Vizier lying in a swoon. The gardener brought water and sprinkled it on the Vizier's face. He also uttered a charm which healed his bruises. Then the Vizier arose and began to weep. "Alas!" he exclaimed. "Would I were dead! The king will cast me in prison when day dawns because his peerless elephant has been slain and devoured. On me will the blame fall, although I am innocent, I will certainly be put to death."

Said the gardener: "When morning comes, go to his Majesty and take with you Hear all and See All, and me also. We shall relate all we have knowledge of, and, if the king wills it, we are ready to die with you."

In the morning the Vizier went before his Majesty, accompanied by the three men.

"Is the elephant safe and well?" the king asked.

Said the Vizier: "Alas! Your Majesty, the elephant has shared the fate of the white camel and the swift-footed steeds."

"Then you will die," thundered the Rajah passionately. "I am now convinced of your guilt and will listen to no explanation." The gardener said: "May it please Your Majesty to her what I have to tell, for I am ready to die with the Vizier if such is your will. If he is guilty, I am guilty; and if he is innocent, I am innocent.

Said the king: "Then speak and I will hear, but be brief."

The gardener and his two helpers each related what and taken place; but his Majesty said: "This is a pretty story. You are all conspirators and will die together. What proof is there, other than your own words, that a Rakshasa accomplished this foul deed?"

See All spoke saying: "I pray your Majesty to hear me. When the Rakshasa had devoured the elephant, it changed its shape and became a bat."

Said the king: "If that was so, why did you not follow the bat and slay it?"

"Because it took refuge in your palace," See All made answer. His Majesty's face was troubled, and he spoke not a word.

Then said the gardener: "Before the Rakshasa ceased devouring the elephant, a spearman wounded it by thrusting his spear through the door. Let search be made through the palace so that it may be found whether one of the inmates is so wounded."

The king looked about him a pondered a while. Then he gave command that all the palace servants should be summoned before him. See All walked round and examined the feet of each servant, but found no wound on any one of them. Then all the guards and all the high officials who slept in the palace were summoned, and the feet of all these were examined, without avail. His Majesty grew impatient, and said to the gardener: "I have borne long with each of you in silence. Now I will summon the guards to seize you all."

Said the gardener: "Let the feet of all the ladies in the palace be examined." The king grew pale, but not with anger so much as fear. He summoned all the ladies, and they come before him, except the chief queen, who sent word by a bondswoman, saying: "What foolishness is this? Is your Majesty the servant of the gardener, who was cast in prison a few days ago?"

The ladies' feet were examined and they were dismissed.

Said the gardener: "I pray your Majesty to command the chief queen to come hither. She cannot transform herself in daytime, so that we have naught to fear."

Said Hear All: "I can hear her limbs trembling; she is afraid."

The king grew paler. For a time he hesitated. Then the gardener said: "If the chief queen is innocent, she has nothing to fear, while we, your humble subjects, know full we that by falsely accusing her we will earn speedy deaths."

Again the king sent for the chief Rani, and again the sent a mocking message of refusal. His Majesty then beckoned to his guards, and they brought the chief queen before him by force. No sooner did she enter the chamber than the king saw a blood-stained bandage round her right foot.

See All tore off the bandage and exclaimed: "Look, your Majesty, have we not spoken truly? This is a spear wound."

The chief queen shrieked and attempted to flee from the palace. But the guards bound her and carried her away, as his Majesty commended. Before night fell she was executed, and so the kingdom was cleared of a false and fierce enemy.

The Vizier was honored by the king, and the gardener was restored to his position and rich gifts of gold. Hear All and See All were installed as watchmen in the palace, and if they are not yet dead, they both live happily and fare well.

OLD MOTHER STAR AND HER CHILDREN

Old Mother Star lives at the very highest point in the sky, and never moves. The Sun and the Moon and the Wind are her children. A long time ago when these three were young they were invited to a grand feast, which was given by Thunder, their aunt. Poor old Mother Star could not go with them. She had to sit patiently in her place all night and required sleep during the daytime. Besides, she had grown very frail.

The children enjoyed the feast, because many rare and sweet dainties were provided for them. Both the Sun and the Wind were greedy and selfish, and they ate and ate and seemed never to be satisfied. Nor did they ever think of anyone except themselves. But the soft-hearted Moon was different from these two. She was sorry her mother could not come to enjoy the nice food, and before she began to take some for herself, she gathered the sweetest bits together and placed them in her little basket, so that she might convey them to the highest point in the sky.

When the feast was over, the children turned their faces homeward. The Sun went first, racing fast with a hot face and the Wind scampered along, panting and blowing and blustering about, sometimes falling and then rising suddenly, sometimes walking sedately and never pausing, except when she stooped down behind a mountain to tie the laces of her silver shoes.

When the Sun reached home his mother said: "I am sure there were more dainties at the feast than you were able to eat. Did you bring something for me?"

Said the Sun: "No, indeed! I went to uncle and aunt's fine feast to enjoy myself. I didn't go to fetch food for my old mother."

The Wind arrived soon afterwards, and Mother Star asked: "What have you brought home for me?"

Said the wind: "Why ask me such a question? I went out to make merry and have a good time. You never asked me to bring anything home."

Old Mother Star said nothing. She waited until the pretty Moon came towards her, smiling softly. But before she could ask a single question, her daughter spoke sweetly saying: "My little basket is full of dainties, Mother. I have brought them home for you from the feast." Then she emptied out her store of gifts so that the poor old StaR might enjoy herself, although she was unable to take a holiday.

Soon afterward Mother Star called her children and said: "The time has come for you to leave my home and go your own ways. Hear my parting words."

She first addressed the Sun, saying: "You were fed by me when you were a babe, and I protected you against all evil. My heart was always devoted to you. I suffered for your sake; I hungered for your sake. But you went away to the grand feast of Thunder and Lightning, and thought of no one but yourself. All you troubled about was to find selfish enjoyment. You did not remember your poor old Mother, who could not leave home, and was so hungry and frail. Therefore you must be punished. Your face will ever remain hot and burning. The rays falling from you upon the earth will scorch everyone, and, as you rise higher and higher in the sky, you will torment mankind so much that they will dislike you and hide themselves from you; they will never say a kind word about you."

That is how the face of the Sun is still burning hot. Often, too, before it goes home for the night, it blushes with shame, remembering what Mother Star said.

Mother Star next addressed the Wind, saying: "Like the Sun, you have been very unkind. I was hungry and you did not bring me food. I was thirsty and you did not bring me a cool grape. Therefore when the Sun dries the world with its burning face, you will run fastest and blow hardest, feeling thirsty yourself: you will also dry up everything you touch."

That is why the Wind is miserable and hated in hot weather.

Mother Star spoke next to the Moon, saying: "You are my

soft-eyed and faithful daughter. Before you ate anything at the feast you laid aside a portion for me, remembering that I was hungry and old and frail. You did so because you love me. Now you will receive my blessing. You will ever be gentle and fair and smiling. Your light will not burn anyone. It will be cool and pleasant, and refreshing. Mankind will ever praise you and love you, and you will be their guide on long journeys. You will measure out the months and the years. You will measure out the lives of all. You will bring increase to everything. You will cause the seeds to sprout in the ground, and you will ripen the harvest of grain and fruit. Everyone will bless you and you will always be happy."

That is why the Moon shines soft and cool by night, and is ever so calm and beautiful and tender.